AF604778

ABOUT THE AUTHOR

His Holiness the Dalai Lama is the spiritual leader of the Tibetan people and head of the Tibetan government-in-exile. His tireless efforts on behalf of human rights, world peace, and basic human values have brought him international recognition. A recipient of the Nobel Peace Prize, he travels the world speaking on peace, giving Buddhist teachings and meeting with political leaders, as he works tirelessly for Tibet.

For more information about the Dalai Lama, including his schedule of teachings, visit: www.dalailama.com.

LIGHTING THE PATH

LIGHTING THE PATH

HIS HOLINESS
THE
DALAI LAMA

EDITED AND TRANSLATED BY
GESHE THUPTEN JINPA

First published in Australia and New Zealand in 2003
by Thomas C. Lothian Pty Ltd
(an imprint of Hachette Australia Pty Limited)
Level 17, 207 Kent Street, Sydney NSW 2000
www.hachette.com.au

This edition published in 2019

10 9 8 7 6 5 4 3 2 1

A catalogue record for this
book is available from the
National Library of Australia

ISBN: 978 0 7336 4195 4 (hardback)

Cover design by Luke Causby, Blue Cork Designs
Cover photograph courtesy of Alamy
Text design by Caz Brown
Printed and bound in Australia by McPherson's Printing Group

The paper this book is printed on is certified against the Forest Stewardship Council® Standards. McPherson's Printing Group holds FSC® chain of custody certification SA-COC-005379. FSC® promotes environmentally responsible, socially beneficial and economically viable management of the world's forests.

Contents

Foreword

Lighting the Path: The Dalai Lama Teaches on Wisdom and Compassion comprises a selection of teachings and talks given by His Holiness the Dalai Lama during his tour of Australia and New Zealand in May 2002. It contains both informal talks to the general public as well as more formal teachings on Buddhist thought and practice.

In the public talks, central themes include practical ways in which we can increase our warm-heartedness towards others and develop a positive attitude to life; and ways to transform adverse situations into conditions favourable to spiritual development and a happier life. There is also an engaging discussion between His Holiness and young people. Specially targeted events allowed school students and young adults to speak directly to His Holiness and ask him questions on a whole range of issues, from inner peace to social change.

At the heart of this book are three more formal Buddhist teachings. The chapter, 'Principles of Buddhism', provides the framework for understanding Buddha Shakyamuni's first and fundamental teaching on the Four Noble Truths, upon which all his other teachings are based. The next chapter, 'Eight Verses on Mind Training', is centred around Geshe Langri Thangpa's *Eight Verses on Training the Mind*, which is part of a genre of Tibetan spiritual writings known as *lojong* (literally 'training the mind'). His Holiness often refers to this short work as one of his main sources of inspiration for the practice of compassion.

The longest and perhaps the most profound teaching in this work is His Holiness' commentary to Atisha Dipamkara's *Lamp for the Path to Enlightenment*, which he gave over three days in Melbourne. The remarkable Indian meditator and teacher Atisha Dipamkara settled in Tibet later in his life, where he made a significant contribution to the establishment and flourishing of Buddhist thought and practice. This particular work has become one of the most important texts for serious practitioners of Buddhism, and we are supremely fortunate to have it so lucidly and inspiringly explained to us by His Holiness the Dalai Lama. In this context, we would like to express our gratitude to Geshe Thupten Jinpa for his brilliant translation of His Holiness' teachings into English.

The Tibet Information Office in Canberra had the great privilege of co-ordinating this memorable visit of His Holiness the Dalai Lama to the Antipodes, which was jointly organised by the Dalai Lama in Australia Limited and the Dalai Lama Charitable Trust New Zealand. These two non-profit organisations were especially established to manage His Holiness the Dalai Lama's visits to this part of the world, and we were deeply impressed by the sincerity and dedication of their members and the thousands of volunteers who assisted them. We would like to express our gratitude to them all. We also extend our thanks to Geshe Sonam Thargye, a Tibetan monk residing in Geelong, Victoria, who initiated His Holiness' visit to Australia on this occasion.

The venues for His Holiness' teachings and public talks were always full, and since his visit many members of the public have expressed an interest in gaining access to the teachings and talks in written form. Therefore, we are very happy to witness the publication of this book and we offer our thanks to all those involved in its compilation and publication. We have no doubt that it will be of great benefit to many people.

Chope Paljor Tsering
Representative of His Holiness the Dalai Lama
for Australia and New Zealand, 1998–2003

1
Our Quest for Happiness

EVERYONE WANTS A HAPPY, PEACEFUL LIFE AND TO LIVE IN a happy world. I believe this is our basic purpose and right and something really worth making an effort to achieve worldwide. We don't need to talk about this in purely philosophical terms. Whether or not we have a clear awareness of what the 'self' is, we all know that we experience pleasure and pain, that we want happiness and do not want suffering.

The basic desire for happiness, peace and pleasure,

and the equally basic desire to overcome pain and suffering are just naturally there in all of us. I come from Tibet, which some people consider to be a mysterious land they call 'Shangri-la'. And some people even describe me as a 'living Buddha' or a 'god-king'. These are all nonsense! Actually, we human beings are all the same, mentally, emotionally and physically. Your feelings and emotions are the same as mine.

As a simple Buddhist monk, a practitioner of the teachings of the Buddha, and as a human being, I am seriously concerned about our human problems, because every human being has responsibility and should care for our planet and its inhabitants. Many of the problems we are facing today are essentially man-made. Although our world has changed a lot, I believe that we tend to handle problems in an outdated fashion and that this can create more problems and more conflict.

For example, events that occurred in the eighteenth and nineteenth centuries would have been unlikely to have much effect upon a distant continent. But today's world is heavily interdependent as a result of such factors as technology, population growth and globalisation. So, in my view, making our own country's interests top priority at the expense of others can have serious consequences.

Instead, we must think of humanity as a whole and have a sense of concern at the global level. I call this having a sense of 'universal responsibility'.

There are some problems in life which we simply cannot avoid, and in such cases our own mental attitude is very important. For instance, we have a body and so we have to face the inevitable problems associated with sickness, ageing and death. No one has yet discovered a method whereby we can overcome these factors. Then, because we live in a human society, we are bound to experience some disagreements and difficulties from time to time. Even within our own family (or within ourself) there can be opposing ideas and views, which can cause conflict to arise. There is nothing wrong with contradiction in itself. Movement arises in the world of matter from opposing forces and energies. Similarly, conflict in the area of ideas and opinions can bring about new and meaningful debates and findings. In fact, contradiction is part of nature.

What is important is how we relate to contradictions and whether we can use them positively. This is why our mental attitude is the key. If we can sustain peace in our own mind, even apparently hostile forces or events will not throw us off balance. On the other hand, if our mind is very agitated and disturbed we will not experience genuine peace and contentment, even if we have the best material facilities and our closest friends around us.

As I mentioned earlier, I believe that our basic purpose and right is to have a happy life — and not just we human beings but also all species of animal, bird and insect. One remarkable thing about human beings is our intelligence. There are so many different forms of life on this planet, and especially many forms of life with a mind. But I think only we humans really change this world through our scientific discoveries and other new developments.

Much of humanity today enjoys quite a high level of material facilities and, with the help of science and technology, further developments will take place. At one time it may have seemed possible that material facilities and progress could overcome all the difficulties of daily life, so that all suffering would disappear and humanity could achieve some kind of permanent happiness. But as time goes on we see many people enjoying the very best material facilities and yet we cannot say that they have no problems or suffering. I have met some people who are even millionaires or billionaires, but when they tell me about their lives it is clear that they have a lot of worry and mental unrest. I advise them to try to practise contentment, and then to think more about other people and look at their own life from a wider perspective. Sometimes this advice helps them and they find a new way to view their own problems. This shows that material facilities alone cannot provide genuine happiness or success. So much depends on our own attitude.

I'm not saying that material facilities are not important, because obviously they are important. As a monk I am prohibited from wearing jewellery, but I do have a watch. Of course, it is not just an ornament but also has a practical purpose. And although it's not very expensive, it's also not very cheap! Material facilities are beneficial and practical, and there's no problem with this. The problem comes when they create feelings of greed, competitiveness and some kind of enduring dissatisfaction, which makes us want more and more.

While material facilities provide us with physical comforts, many of our feelings of pleasure and pain are actually created by the mind itself. When we examine the world of experience, we see two broad categories. One category relates to those experiences of happiness and suffering which are at the level of our senses, while the other category is primarily related to our thoughts and emotions. In the case of suffering related to sensory experience, the remedy comes from that same source — for instance, we cure physical illness with medicine. But on the mental level, sufferings such as worry and suspicion eventually cause depression. If the depression becomes very serious, then it becomes closely connected to the physical body also. But basically many of these mental states are created by the mind itself, and so material facilities cannot bring about a change. Money, power, fame — nothing in the material world can eliminate suffering which is on a purely mental level.

In order to overcome this kind of suffering, we need a different method. The problems we encounter in our life as a result of our thoughts and emotions need to be resolved by using the same mental faculty which creates our thoughts and emotions. Perhaps because of this marvellous human intelligence, we human beings have more mental problems. When animals have fed well and there is no immediate threat in their environment, they seem to have few worries. But for us, even though for the moment everything is very comfortable, our mind creates the disturbances of too much expectation or doubt and concerns for our long-term future and the future generations.

Sometimes we have too much imagination! So on one hand human intelligence is something very precious, but on the other hand that precious intelligence is the very source of many of our problems.

To overcome our mental sufferings we need to use the same mental faculty that creates thoughts and emotions to resolve the problems they cause. In other words, we need to use our intelligence. Neither belief, nor faith, nor prayer can do it. In the beginning we use analysis at the intellectual level to look into the various causes and factors of the particular problem we face. This helps us to arrive at a certain understanding of the way things are. Then, through a process of familiarising ourselves with this understanding and integrating it into our life, we reach a point where it becomes almost second nature to not only have an intellectual understanding but also an experiential understanding of that truth.

This is how we can use our intelligence to transform our mind, by shaping the right kind of mental attitude. But I think emotion is the principal factor here, because the right kind of emotions really help to build our strength of mind. The application of intelligence or wisdom is the method we use to discriminate between useful and harmful emotions. Most people tend to think that emotions are something negative. For example, when someone is described as 'too emotional', this is a pejorative term; but I feel this attitude is incorrect because there are both positive and negative emotions. A sense of caring for others and affection are positive emotions, which are very useful. In contrast, hatred, fear and pride are obviously negative emotions because they create discomfort in our own mind and the minds of others.

Once again we need to use our intelligence here, as we learn to discriminate between useful and harmful emotions. It is important to gain a clear awareness and conviction that such emotions as hatred and greed are destructive inner forces that we can work to reduce and ultimately overcome. Otherwise we may have the impression that, although these negative emotions are destructive, they are a natural part of our mind and as such there's not much we can do about them. But when we realise their destructive nature, this in itself gradually reduces their force or power. According to my own experience, the study and analysis I have done through analytical meditation, into ill-feeling towards others and other negative emotions, has completely convinced me that these emotions are the real enemy that disturbs our inner peace and happiness.

For example, anger often seems to be our protector or trusted friend. Also, when we are arguing with someone, anger appears to give us more energy and strength to fight back. But if we analyse properly, the energy brought on by anger is what I call 'blind energy'. It often results in destruction or even self-destruction, because the best part of our brain cannot function properly while very strong anger is dominant. Instead, we just see the short-term rather than the long-term interest or consequences. This is why I say that such outbursts of anger are 'blind'. Sometimes, as a joke, I mention one driver I had in Lhasa in 1959. This man was bald and he was very short-tempered. One day, as he was doing some repair work underneath the car, he somehow hit his head which made him lose his temper. In his rage he then hit the car with his hand, which only caused him more suffering. If we use our common sense, we know that when human flesh hits metal, the flesh will suffer, not the metal.

In my own case also, in Tibet I had a pocket watch that didn't work well. I opened its back and moved one small part of it, trying to make it work again. When it still failed to work, I lost my temper and hit it on the table, which only broke it completely. I think most of us have had a similar experience, so we know the destructive outcome of anger that blinds our intelligence or judgement.

If we look at the opposite of anger, which is peace of mind, we can see that no matter how powerful our external enemies may be, they have no ability to directly destroy our peace of mind. But we can destroy it very easily through our negative emotions. When strong anger arises, peace of mind automatically reduces or disappears altogether. When strong attachment arises, peace of mind diminishes; and fear has the same effect.

Of course, some types of fear are justified, such as the fear of having an accident in a car when the road conditions are very bad. This realistic fear of danger is good, because it makes us take more care. Anger can be similar in that it can arise out of a sense of concern for others; that anger is generally positive, whereas the anger that occurs from ill-feeling towards others is negative.

We can apply the same reasoning to the egoistic attitude, the feeling of 'I', which also is of two kinds. One strong sense of 'I' leads people to harm, exploit and abuse others in the pursuit of fulfilling their own interests. This is obviously bad. But the opposite sense of 'I' causes people to willingly experience difficulties and even sacrifice their own position and privileges out of a sense of concern for others and a desire to help them. It gives them a kind of self-confidence that they can and should act for the sake of others. On the basis of will-power and determination that strong sense of 'I' is positive.

So I think we need to make a clear distinction between positive and negative emotions. Some emotions may be considered intrinsically hostile or negative, but if they are motivated by more positive emotions such as compassion, they can be transformed into a positive force or energy. Let's take one example here. Let's say you have a neighbour who is unfriendly and wants to create a little trouble for you. His antagonistic attitude causes you to develop some feeling of ill-will towards him. This feeling nags at you constantly and as a result your mood becomes uncomfortable and difficult. The first casualty is not your neighbour but your own family members, including your children, who suffer from your unhappy mood. You feel frustrated every time your family approaches you, and sometimes you express this frustration by shouting at them. Eventually your friends, who often used to call on you, stop coming because of your bad mood. Without your usual friendly visitors and good family atmosphere, you become even unhappier. You keep your curtains closed and remain in your room like a virtual prisoner. You take tranquillisers, sleeping pills and alcohol, and gradually your physical condition deteriorates and the genuine smile on your face completely vanishes. Now, if your neighbour really wishes harm on you, he hasn't had to do a thing, has he? You have fulfilled his desire for him. Your own anger and hatred have destroyed your good fortune.

But if despite your neighbour's negative attitude towards you, you remain calm and happy, your friendly visitors come and go, you and your family go on picnics and take holidays, your work carries on successfully and your good fortune increases, eventually your neighbour may feel a little worried! Furthermore, if necessary, you can take a counter-measure by using your legal system. In that way you can beat your neighbour through reasoning, without negative emotions and, if possible, out of a genuine concern for him — because if you allow him to continue to take advantage of you unreasonably, he will gradually spoil his life. So out of concern for him and respect for justice, you can take a counter-measure. If we analyse in this way, we slowly develop a clear conviction that hatred is really bad, both for oneself and for others.

According to medical science, a frustrated mind, fear, stress and anger are all very bad for our health. At a seminar on human health that I attended, one doctor presented statistics which showed that people who often use the words 'I', 'me' and 'mine' are in more danger of suffering from a heart attack than others. I think the logic behind this is that when we think more about others, our mind and perspective are widened and our own problems appear less significant. The problems remain the same but our attitude changes so that we feel, 'I can manage.' Conversely, an extremely self-centred attitude keeps our mind very narrow, and in that small space our problems appear to be really unbearable.

So how should we confront our negative emotions? Let's take anger as an example. Some anger is very forceful and some less so. When it is relatively mild, as it is about to arise we can try to see the aggravating situation from a different angle and this may bring some positive outlook. In my own case, I lost my country and became a refugee, which was extremely unfortunate in many respects. But, looking at it another way, it has brought me more opportunity to meet different people and freely exchange views with them without the constraints of formal protocols. So we can use this method of considering the situation from every angle and look for the positive side to try to halt mild anger in its tracks and overcome it that way. However, dealing with strong anger is much more difficult, because when it has a hold on our mind it is almost impossible to control it or make it go away. The only effective method is to work with our mind while it is free from strong emotion, analysing our inner world over and over again and gradually developing more awareness and some new convictions. In this way, we develop a healthier mind and body. Then when the negative emotions arise they are weaker. This is a way of training the mind. Some people go to great lengths to change their physical shape. I think that this way of training our mind is rather like making a new shape for our emotions.

Here again there is a certain similarity between our physical well-being and our mental well-being. If our basic physical constitution is strong and our basic health is sound, then even if we face some illnesses, our body is able to resist and overcome these. In the same manner, a basically sound and ethical outlook prevents many negative thoughts and emotions from arising. And even when they do occur, because our outlook and way of thinking is sound, we are well-equipped to overcome them and they don't have a lasting impact on us. Then, in the future, we will be able to reduce their occurrence.

For such a transformation to take place at the mental level, and especially at the emotional level, time is a major factor. We need to engage in constant effort, such as analytical meditation, so that gradually we familiarise ourselves and gain conviction and more determination. It is misguided and unrealistic to think that just one thought will remove a negative emotion for good, as if we were taking a painkiller to cure a headache. Transforming the mind takes time.

At sixteen years of age I lost my freedom and at the age of twenty-four I lost my country. I have been a political refugee for more than 43 years now. In the meantime, news from Tibet is always very sad. Throughout this period of time I have found one of the most reliable supporters or protectors has been my own intelligence; a combination of 'brain' and 'heart'. This gives me inner strength, self-confidence and enthusiasm. In spite of many problems I never touch tranquillisers and, of course, as a monk I cannot drink alcohol — but there is also no need for these, nor for sleeping pills! In my daily life I sometimes receive disturbing or even heartbreaking news, or hear of some tragic situation. Naturally I feel a lot of sadness and sometimes even anger on a superficial level, but these emotions don't remain with me for long. Deep inside I have some kind of peace of mind. I call this the combination of 'intelligence' and 'good heart', and I think this is a real help. My case is not unique; everyone has the same potential. The question is whether we develop our potential or not.

As human beings we are born and grow up under the affection of our parents, so from childhood we learn the value of human affection and kindness. Modern medical science holds the view that physical touch by our mother or carer from the very beginning of our life is a crucial factor in our development. People everywhere now realise the importance of education, but not everyone pays adequate attention to the development of a warm heart. I like to ask people to think more about the human values: compassion, affection and a sense of caring for one another. If we acquire more of such values our feelings and emotions will be healthier, and as a result we will have more peace of mind. Then, when we face problems, we can handle them more easily. Whereas if our mind is too disturbed by emotions, even simple problems will be very difficult to solve because we cannot use our intelligence properly. Each of us has the potential to develop a warm human heart. People often think that practising compassion and forgiveness brings benefit to others and additional misery to oneself, but I think this attitude is mistaken. The benefit actually goes to the practitioner, not the recipient.

I can illustrate this with one small example from my own life. I recently developed an intestinal infection that was very painful. While I was ill, I passed through some villages near Patna in Bihar, one of India's poorest states. I saw many children on the road, some of whom were sick and some polio patients, and it seemed as though no one was taking care of them. There was also an old man lying in a small shack, he looked very sick but no one was looking after him. I felt really moved. All day and night in my mind's eye I kept seeing these poor children and that old man. This reduced the feeling of my own pain, my own sickness. Some compassion for them constantly diverted my mind, and as a result my pain was lessened. A greater sense of concern about others actually strengthens one's own inner being. The illness didn't disappear because of the compassion, but at least the painful feelings and the mental anxiety associated with them were greatly reduced.

If just one member of a family has a really good heart, then the whole family, neighbours and general community benefit. So if we really wish to strive for our goal of a happy world, we should put effort into developing our own good heart in combination with intelligence. Then a happier, more harmonious, friendly and peaceful society can develop.

These days, it seems that people and governments everywhere fully realise the importance of education. But their focus seems to be on developing the brain and they do not pay much attention to the other side — by which I mean our emotions, our warm heart and basic human values. Traditionally these were the province of religious institutions. In today's society, however, the influence of these institutions and of family values is decreasing and, as a result, it seems that nobody is taking care of younger people's basic human values. In my view, family members, educational institutions and the media all have a special role to play in this regard.

We should not underestimate the importance of these good human values, both for our society and for ourselves. For example, we cannot develop genuine, meaningful spiritual experiences without good human qualities as our foundation. In this respect each individual is responsible for himself and herself and no one can develop our good heart for us. But each of us has the same potential to create a happy life.

I think people in modern times pay too much attention to external things and not enough attention to investigating deeply their own inner world. So one request or suggestion I have is to think more about your inner world. Naturally you need to attend to your work and other responsibilities. But in the early morning or late evening, or whenever you have some leisure time, look deeply into your mind and emotions.

Don't think that such an activity is purely something to do with religion. Religious faith is different. The main method in Buddhism is to change or shape our emotions through reasoning, using our intelligence. So I think we can adopt some of these Buddhist methods in the secular world. Without needing any religious or specifically Buddhist belief, others can test the effectiveness of these methods for themselves.

I always make it clear that I'm not interested in propagating Buddhism. Religious faith and practice are an individual's right. But I do think that many people should make more effort to develop a warm heart, because this is the seed of our happiness and of our future. The future of humanity entirely depends upon us. Prayer may have some effect, but the real effect must come from our hard work, with sincere motivation and clear vision.

2
Principles of Buddhism

I SHALL PRESENT HERE A BRIEF SUMMARY OF THE CONCEPTUAL framework underpinning the Buddha's fundamental teaching on the Four Noble Truths — the truth of suffering, the truth of its origin, the truth of its cessation, and the truth of the path leading to cessation.

The Buddha taught these noble truths soon after his attainment of enlightenment as part of what is known as the first turning of the Wheel of Dharma. Without a good understanding of the Four Noble Truths we cannot proceed meaningfully in our study and understanding of the nature of reality according to Buddhism. But first, I would like to make it clear that all major religious traditions have the same potential, the same message and goal, by which I mean the genuine wish to bring about better world conditions, a happier world with a more compassionate humanity. This is what all the major religions share.

In order to live harmoniously, we must make a common effort. It is very important to have mutual respect, rather than trying to propagate your own tradition. Therefore I always emphasise that people from different traditions should keep their own faith and not be in a hurry to change their religion. There are many Asian people in Australia today who come from traditionally Buddhist countries, and in this gathering here we have monks and nuns from Vietnam, Thailand, Burma, Sri Lanka and Japan; in addition there are those from China, Mongolia and Tibet. Also, there are some people among the millions of Westerners of traditionally Christian backgrounds who have an inclination or mental attitude which finds the Buddhist approach more effective. On that basis I am giving some explanation about the Dharma here today.

Three levels of understanding

In Buddhism, one speaks of three different levels of understanding, which are sequential — an understanding arrived at through learning and studying, an understanding developed as a result of deep reflection and contemplation, and an understanding acquired through meditative experience.

There is a definite order in the sequence of this three. So on the basis of study and learning — which is the first level — we deepen our understanding of a given topic by constantly reflecting upon it until we arrive at a point where we gain a high degree of certainty or conviction that is firmly grounded in reason. At this point, even if others were to contradict our understanding and the premises upon which it is based we would not be swayed, because our conviction in the truth has arisen through the power of our own critical reflection. This is the second level of understanding which, however, is still at the level of the intellect. If we pursue this understanding further and deepen it through constant contemplation and familiarity with the truth, we reach a point where we feel the impact at the emotional level. In other words, our conviction is no longer at the level of mere intellect. This is the third level of understanding, which is experiential, and this is referred to in the Buddhist texts as an understanding derived through meditative experience.

Once you have listened to my presentation, many of you may acquire the first level of understanding. If you become interested in the topic of the Four Noble Truths, you will then need to build upon this first level of understanding by constantly familiarising yourself with it through deep reflection and contemplation. So, in a sense, you have to do your homework! You can then reach the second level of understanding.

For those among you who are genuinely interested in the Buddhist teachings and the spiritual path they present, you will need to deepen your understanding still further by engaging in regular meditation so that you can progress to the third level of understanding. You need to appreciate, however, that this process will take time. It requires commitment to a long and sustained period of spiritual practice. So you may need to overcome the modern-day habit of automation. We flick a switch and something pops up! We need to strive to overcome this conditioning and go back through more than 2000 years of human endeavour, to a time when hard work was the only viable method.

Buddhism and other ancient Indian traditions

More than 2500 years ago, before Buddha Shakyamuni was born, various spiritual and philosophical systems of thought existed in India. The Buddha integrated in his own teachings some of the themes and practices of these systems of thought, such as the cultivation of single-pointedness of mind to develop calm abiding, and various meditation practices aimed at reducing the levels of attachment. On the basis of these and other spiritual teachings, the Buddha developed a unique system of thought and practice centred on the key insight that there is no independently existing or 'real' self. This is the teaching on no-self, known in Sanskrit as *anatman*.

Broadly speaking, there were two main categories within the world of spiritual traditions in ancient India. On one side were the spiritual traditions which, in one form or another, upheld a belief in the concept of a transcendent being or god as a divine creator; while on the other side were traditions which did not subscribe to this concept of a transcendent god. Similarly, some accepted the notion of rebirth or reincarnation, while others did not. Among those which accepted the notion of rebirth, some also accepted the possibility of attaining liberation from cyclic existence and thus the possibility that individuals can find ultimate spiritual freedom. Furthermore, among these, some accepted the notion of an eternal, abiding self (*atman* in Sanskrit) while others rejected this notion of an eternal self. Buddhism belongs to the category of those ancient Indian schools that reject any notion of a transcendent god as creator. Others in this category include a sub-school of the classical Indian Samkhya School, and Jainism.

There was such a tremendous diversity of traditions in ancient India, many of which upheld distinct and, in some cases, conflicting philosophical and metaphysical views. The question is, why was this so? I think it is important to realise that the diversity of traditions, and particularly the metaphysical views underpinning these traditions, really reflects the need of a diverse group of individual practitioners for spiritual solace. This in turn points to the fundamental diversity that naturally exists in the mental dispositions and spiritual inclinations of sentient beings.

Now, as then, the concept of a transcendent god as creator has a powerful and inspiring impact on the lives of those who believe in it. The sense that their entire destiny lies in the hands of an all-powerful, omniscient and compassionate being leads them to try to understand the workings and key message of this transcendent being. Then, when they come to realise that this transcendent being embodies love and infinite compassion, they try to cultivate love and compassion towards their fellow beings as the qualities through which to express love for their creator. They also gain confidence and inspiration through a sense of intimacy or connectedness to this loving, transcendent being.

Although, metaphysically speaking, Buddhists reject any notion of a transcendent creator or god, some individual Buddhists do relate to certain higher beings, such as the goddess Tara, as an independent and real being with power over their destiny. For these practitioners Tara is their sole refuge, their greatest object of veneration and their trusted guardian and protector. What this suggests is that the inclination to seek refuge in an external source is something deeply natural for us as human beings.

But it is also clear that for other people the metaphysical concept of a transcendent being is unacceptable. Questions form in their minds, such as: who created the creator — in other words — where does the transcendent being come from? And how can we posit a true beginning? People with this type of mental disposition look elsewhere for explanations. The ancient Indian Samkhya philosophy, for example, accords with Buddhist thought in accepting that all things and events, including sentient beings, come into existence as a result of causes and conditions. The Samkhya philosophers asserted that reality exists at two levels: there is the world of everyday experience, which is characterised by diversity and plurality; and there is the source of this world of multiplicity, which they called the 'primal substance' (*prakrit* in Sanskrit). Buddhism rejects this theory of reality, instead upholding the understanding that all things and events, including sentient beings, exist merely in dependence upon the aggregation of causes and effects.

Buddhism recognises two general realms of causation: external and internal. The external realm of causation refers to the external environment, such as the whole of our natural environment — that is, the physical world in which we live, including our body. The internal realm of causation constitutes our perceptions, feelings, emotions and thoughts, which we normally label the domain of 'subjective experience'. Both realms of causation are comprised of elements that are transient. In other words, they come into being and at some point they cease to exist. We can observe this transient nature for ourselves, both in our own thoughts and emotions as well as in our natural environment. When we understand this reality we can deduce that, for something to cease to exist, the causes of its cessation must be occurring on a moment-by-moment basis. Nothing else could coherently account for the changes we perceive over a period of time.

In summary, the basic Buddhist viewpoint with regard to the origin and nature of reality is that things and events come into being purely on the basis of the coming together of causes and conditions, and that all such phenomena are transient in that they are subject to constant, moment-by-moment change.

Dependent origination and the law of causality

A key principle here is dependent origination. This fundamental principle of Buddhism states that everything arises and ceases in dependence upon causes and conditions. The fourth-century Indian Buddhist thinker Asanga identified three key conditions governing this principle of dependent origination. First is 'the absence of designer condition', which pertains to the issue of whether or not there is a transcendent intelligence behind the origin of the universe. Second is 'the condition of impermanence', which relates to the notion that the very causes and conditions that give rise to the world of dependent origination are themselves impermanent and subject to change. Third is 'the condition of potentiality'. This very important principle in Buddhist thought refers to the fact that something cannot be produced from just anything. Rather, for a particular set of causes and conditions to give rise to a particular set of effects or consequences, there must be some kind of natural relationship between them.

For example, our internal realm of experience — consisting of our perceptions, intentions, thoughts, emotions and so on — are mental rather than physical phenomena, and therefore we must be able to trace their evolution back through successive stages of mental cognition. We could say that, according to Buddhist understanding, this is part of a natural law that applies equally to the physical world. We must be able to trace the causation of physical properties back to other levels of these properties, and eventually to the beginning of the present universe.

Through this reductive process we can envision a kind of state at the beginning of the present universe where there was a cause for the evolution of the entire macroscopic world. From the Buddhist point of view — for example, in one of the texts of the Kalachakra Tantra — there is an understanding of what are called 'space particles', for want of a better word. These are thought to be extremely subtle material particles which are seen as the source or origin of the entire evolution of the physical universe that we experience now. So in terms of causation we can trace all material objects back to their constituted particle level and, from there, back to the origin of the universe.

The essential point about this condition of potentiality is that, although there is a causal relationship between the physical world and the world of mental phenomena, in terms of their own continuum one cannot be said to be the cause of the other. A mental phenomenon, such as a thought or an emotion, must come from a preceding mental phenomenon; likewise, a particle of matter must come from a preceding particle of matter.

Of course, there is an intimate relationship between the two. We know that mental states can influence material phenomena, such as the body; and, similarly, that material phenomena can act as contributory factors for certain subjective experiences. This is something that we can observe in our lives. Much of our gross level of consciousness is very closely connected to our body, and in fact we often use terminology and conventions which reflect this. For example, when we say 'human mind' or 'human consciousness' we are using the human body as the basis to define a particular mind state. Likewise, at the gross levels of mind such as our sensory experiences, it is very obvious that these are heavily dependent upon our body and some physiological states. When a part of our body is hurt or damaged, for instance, we immediately experience the impact on our mental state. Nevertheless, the principle remains that mental phenomena must come from preceding phenomena of the same kind, and so on.

If we trace mental phenomena back far enough, as in the case of an individual's life, we come to the first instant of consciousness in this life. Once we have traced its continuum to this point of beginning, we then have three options: we can either say that the first instant of consciousness in this life must come from a preceding instant of consciousness which existed in the previous life. Or we can say that this first instant of consciousness came from nowhere — it just sort of 'popped up'. Or we can say that it came from a material cause. From the Buddhist point of view, the last two alternatives are deeply problematic. The Buddhist understanding is that, in terms of its continuum, consciousness or mind is beginningless.

Mental phenomena are beginningless. Therefore, the person or the being — which is essentially a designation based on the continuum of the mind — is also devoid of beginning.

The inner world of consciousness

When we use such terms as 'consciousness' or 'mind' it often tends to give the impression that we are talking about a single, monolithic entity; but this is misleading. Our own personal experience reveals that the mental world is tremendously diverse. Moreover, when we examine each moment of cognition or mental experience, we realise that they all relate to either internal or external objects. For example, if we examine a moment of perception we find that it takes on an aspect of whatever object happens to be its focus in that very moment. And since we often form false impressions based on distorted perceptions, we can say that some of our perceptions are valid while others are not.

Broadly speaking, we can identify two principal categories within the realm of consciousness — that is, our subjective world of experience. There are those that relate to sensory experiences, such as seeing and hearing, where the engagement with objects is direct and unmediated; and there are those where our cognitive engagement with the world is mediated via language, concepts and thoughts. In this model, perception is primarily understood as a direct experience of objects at the sensory level. This occurs through the mediation of sense data but involves no judgement about whether the object is desirable or undesirable, attractive or unattractive, good or bad. These judgements occur at the second stage when conceptual thought comes into play.

Let us now relate this to our personal experience. When we look at something, in that first instant of perception we have a direct, unmediated visual experience of the object. If we then close our eyes and think about the same object we still have its image in our mind, but now we are engaging with it at the level of conceptual thought. These two experiences are qualitatively different, in the sense that the conceptually created image involves conflation of both time and space.

For instance, you see a beautiful flower in one corner of a garden. The next day, you see the same species of flower in another part of the same garden and you think to yourself, 'Oh, I have seen that flower before.' In reality, however, these two flowers are completely distinct and exist in different parts of the garden. Also, the flower you saw yesterday is not the flower you are seeing today. So although these two flowers were separated in terms of space and time, when the moment occurs in your thoughts you are conflating both time and space and projecting the image of the flower that you saw yesterday onto what you are seeing now. This blending of both time and space in our thoughts, which is often mediated through language and concepts, again suggests that some of our perceptions are valid and others are false.

If it were simply the case that these distorted or false perceptions had no negative consequences, this would be fine. But it is not so. Our distorted way of understanding the world leads to all kinds of problems by creating confusion in our mind. This confusion influences the way in which we engage with the world, which in turn causes suffering both for ourselves and for others. Since we naturally wish to be happy and to overcome suffering, it is vital to recognise that a fundamental confusion in our understanding of the world (including our own self) lies at the root of much of our suffering and difficulties. Furthermore, since our experiences of happiness and suffering and the fundamental ignorance that lies at the root of our suffering are all mental phenomena, if we genuinely wish to pursue the fulfilment of our natural aspiration to attain happiness and overcome suffering we must come to understand at least the basic workings of our inner world, namely the world of consciousness.

The four principles of reality

Let us return to our discussion of the Buddhist view that all experiences and things come into existence in dependence upon causes and conditions. What does this imply for our own world or experiences, such as the experiences of pain, pleasure, suffering and happiness? Furthermore, since we all possess this natural desire to be happy and to overcome suffering, when we talk about experiencing suffering and happiness we are talking about the world of our own experience. Since experiences are mental phenomena, it becomes crucial for those who genuinely wish to attain happiness and overcome suffering to understand at least the basic workings of their own internal world.

Our experiences of happiness and suffering do not occur for no reason at all. They arise as a result of preceding causes and conditions and the coming together of many different factors. Some of these factors are external but by far the majority are internal — in other words, they are related to our mental world.

Now we might ask: 'What exactly is the nature of these mental phenomena? How can we see or understand the law of causality in relation to our internal world? On what grounds can we accept that material objects possess certain defining characteristics, such as being visible, tangible and so on? And on what grounds can we understand that mental phenomena also possess defining characteristics, such as being free of obstructive, spatial properties, and having the nature of subjective experience? Why is there a continuum of consciousness at all? And why, for that matter, is there a continuum of the material world?'

The Buddhist notion of the four principles of reality may help us address these important philosophical questions. The first is the principle of nature, according to which it is understood that the fact that we exist and that we possess a natural desire to be happy and overcome suffering is simply the way it is. This principle is similar to the idea of a natural law in science, and also relates to the fact that things and events, including sentient beings, all come into existence as a result of causes and conditions. It also extends to the evolution and origin of our current universe. According to this principle, a kind of natural causation process takes place pervasively. We can say, therefore, that the material continuum of the universe consists of objects and events that come into existence through a process of evolution.

We might then ask: 'Is this a purely natural process with no extraneous influences operating? If so, how can we account for the fact that at a certain point the physical universe takes a certain nature and form, so that it has a direct impact upon sentient beings' experience of pain and pleasure? Furthermore, how is it that, through this seemingly natural process, a certain point is reached at which causes and conditions act as a basis for the arising of consciousness and experience?'

From the Buddhist point of view, this is where *karma* comes into the picture. The term 'karma' literally means 'action', and more specifically refers to the process of cause and effect, where the intention of an agent or being is involved. So here karma means an intentional act committed or carried out by a being who possesses a sentient nature and who is also capable of having a sentient experience.

Let's take the example of a flower again to illustrate this point. Generally, when we find a particular flower attractive and admire its scent and beautiful colour, it becomes an object of enjoyment for us; we enjoy the sight of it, its beauty. At the same time, this flower may be a home for many small insects and other biological organisms. In both cases, even though in itself the flower is a non-sentient object, it has an impact on sentient beings' experience of pain and pleasure. So for Buddhists the concept of karma provides a very useful framework for understanding how a non-sentient object, such as a flower, can directly relate to sentient beings' experience.

Having said this, to what extent karma can be seen as having a role in the origination of a particular flower is open to question. Needless to say, there are other questions as well. For example, what causes the petals of one flower to droop and fade in a day or two while others last for a week? Is this purely a function of natural laws, or does karma play a role even at that level of minute causation? All of these remain open questions. It is perhaps because of this kind of difficulty that the Buddhist texts state that only a buddha's omniscient mind can penetrate the subtlest aspects of the workings of karma, and know at the most microscopic level which specific causes and conditions give rise to which specific consequences. At our level, we can only recognise that an intimate relationship exists between the external elements of the material world and the internal elements of our mental world; and, based on that, we can learn to detect varying levels of subtlety within our mental and emotional experiences.

The second principle of reality that is relevant to our present discussion is 'the principle of dependence', which relates to the understanding of cause and effect. On the basis of understanding the principle of nature — the fact that things naturally exist the way they are — we see the operation of the principle of dependence in the interaction of things and events giving rise to the emergence of further things and events. The third principle is 'the principle of function', which gives us an understanding of how different things — such as particles, atoms and other material substances, as well as mental phenomena — have their own individual properties which cause them to function in their own particular way. Finally, on the basis of understanding these three, we can then apply the fourth principle which is 'the principle of valid reasoning'. This enables us to conclude that, given this, that will occur; and, given that, this will occur, and so on. So we Buddhists employ this framework of the four fundamental principles of reality as we attempt to arrive at a clearer understanding of the workings of causes, conditions and their effects.

The Four Noble Truths

If we now focus on the workings of cause and effect in relation to our own existence, naturally we will take our personal experience as the basis for cultivating deeper insight. In this context, the Buddha's teaching on the Four Noble Truths can prove extremely helpful because it relates directly to our own experience, especially to our inborn desire to seek happiness and overcome suffering. In essence, the Buddha's teaching on the Four Noble Truths leads us first to a profound recognition of the nature of suffering; then to the recognition of the origins of suffering; then to a recognition of the possibility of the cessation of suffering; and finally to a recognition of the path that leads to such freedom.

Buddhism recognises three levels of suffering: the suffering of suffering, the suffering of change, and the pervasive suffering of conditioned existence.

With regard to the first of these — the suffering of suffering — even animals are capable of identifying these obviously painful experiences as undesirable. Just like us, they show a natural instinct to avoid and be free of such experiences.

With respect to the second level of suffering — the suffering of change — even non-Buddhist practitioners can successfully cultivate both the recognition that this is undesirable and the desire to gain freedom from it.

It is the suffering of pervasive conditioning that is distinctive to Buddhism. Spiritual practitioners who aspire to seek complete liberation from cyclic existence must develop a profound recognition of this form of suffering. We need to cultivate an understanding that the suffering of pervasive conditioning not only acts as the basis for our present experience of suffering but, crucially, also serves as the source of future experiences of suffering. Based on such a firm recognition of our very conditioned existence as a form of suffering, we must then cultivate the genuine desire to seek freedom. Our sense of yearning for freedom should be so forceful that we feel as if this conditioned existence is an acute illness from which we eagerly wish to recover as quickly as possible.

What gives rise to this third level of suffering, namely the suffering of pervasive conditioning? Buddhism identifies the two factors of karma and afflictions as the true origins of suffering. Karma arises from mental afflictions, which are principally of two types: conceptual afflictions, such as mistaken views, and emotional afflictions such as lust, anger and envy. We refer to these as 'afflictions' (*nyongmong* in Tibetan) because their arising in our heart and mind immediately creates a form of affliction characterised by a state of deep disturbance and unrest. This leads to further levels of affliction in our mind and heart, such as being plagued by sorrow, confusion and other forms of suffering.

Generally, all these mental afflictions arise from the three basic poisons of mind — attachment, anger and delusion. Delusion is the foundation of the other two and of all our afflictions; and, in the context of Mahayana Buddhist thought, delusion refers to our mistaken notion of grasping at the real existence of things and events. So it is through the eradication of delusion — which lies at the root of all afflictions — that we strive to bring about an end to suffering and thereby attain true liberation (*moksha* in Sanskrit).

In his *Fundamentals of the Middle Way*, the influential second-century Buddhist thinker Nagarjuna explains that it is only by cultivating insight into the emptiness of self and phenomena that we can see through our delusions and bring this whole deluded chain of cause and effects to an end. Therefore, the understanding of emptiness combined with the cultivation of compassion is the very essence of the practice of the Buddha's teachings.[1] A realised practitioner, who has actualised the true cessation of suffering, will continue to live out this principle in the world through compassionate action. I describe this as the beautiful activity of someone who has realised emptiness and engages in compassionate behaviour.

The Three Higher Trainings

The teaching on the Four Noble Truths, which was the Buddha's first teaching following his attainment of full awakening, represents the foundation for the practices of emptiness and the cultivation of compassion. This teaching underpins everything that the Buddha taught subsequently and helps us to establish a fundamental understanding of the way that things really are. On the basis of such an understanding we can successfully engage in the practices embodied in the Three Higher Trainings. These are the higher trainings in morality, in concentration and in wisdom. The higher training in morality serves as the foundation for the cultivation of single-pointedness of mind, which is a key component of the second higher training, namely the higher training in concentration.

There are different categories of precepts in the higher training on morality. Broadly speaking, there are the layperson's precepts or morality and the ordained member's precepts or morality. Altogether we can list seven or eight different classes of precepts that combine to embody the teachings on morality. Taking morality or the practice of ethical discipline as a foundation, the individual practitioner cultivates single-pointedness of mind and thus develops the second higher training, which is the higher training in concentration.

The reason why Buddhist texts refer to these three as 'higher trainings' is to distinguish them from ordinary practices of morality, single-pointedness and insight, which by themselves are not unique to Buddhism. What is required in the Buddhist context for such a practice to be considered a higher training is for it to be based on an appropriate motivation, such as seeking refuge in the Three Jewels. The Three Jewels are the Buddha, who is the teacher, the Dharma, which is the teaching, and the Sangha, the community of sincere practitioners. Of these three, a Buddhist practitioner must particularly take refuge in the Dharma as the actual means to end suffering and attain liberation. In addition to going for refuge, a Buddhist practice of developing single-pointedness must be grounded on a deep sense of renunciation transcending all mundane concerns. On the basis of these two —

morality as the basis and single-pointedness as the method — the actual path is enshrined in the higher training of wisdom.

The Buddha's teachings on wisdom are presented in the texts of the first turning of the Wheel of Dharma within the framework of the 'thirty-seven aspects of the path to enlightenment'.[2]

In the teachings of the second turning of the Wheel of Dharma, great emphasis is placed on two essential points of practice: the first of these is *bodhicitta* which is the generation of the altruistic mind of awakening — that is, the intention to attain buddhahood for the benefit of the infinite number of sentient beings — which forms the focus of our later chapter on Langri Thangpa's *Eight Verses on Training the Mind*. The second essential point of practice is the cultivation of a deep insight into the ultimate nature of reality. This refers to the cultivation of a deeper understanding of the third noble truth — the truth of the cessation of suffering. The true nature of cessation refers to cessation of the afflictive emotions and thoughts, which we can achieve as a result of applying the appropriate antidotes or remedies.

If we are to truly understand the cessation of suffering, we first need to recognise what lies at the root of our mental and emotional afflictions, and then learn to discern which states of mind act as direct antidotes to them. Furthermore, we need to investigate whether or not these afflictive emotions and thoughts have any sound basis, and whether or not there is a genuine possibility of uprooting them from our mental continuum. In brief, the teachings of the second turning of the Wheel can be seen as representing further elaborations on the themes presented in the first turning of the Wheel, especially with regard to the third and fourth noble truths — the truth of cessation, and the truth of the path leading to cessation.

As for the third turning of the Wheel of Dharma, a key definitive text belonging to this class is the *Essence of Buddhahood* (*Tathagatagarbha Sutra*), which is the primary source text for Maitreya's well-known work *The Sublime Continuum* (*Uttaratantra*) in which we find a comprehensive discussion of the ultimate nature of mind. The teachings of this turning of the Wheel constitute a very profound understanding of the fourth noble truth, the truth of the path leading to cessation.

These teachings help deepen our understanding of the emptiness of mind as opposed to the emptiness of external objects like vases, pillars and so on. Although both the mind and external objects are empty by nature, there is a vast difference insofar as the impact of understanding their emptiness is concerned. For when we examine the ultimate nature of mind carefully, we find it to be not only empty — that is, devoid of intrinsic reality — but naturally luminous as well. This leads us to realise that all the mental afflictions that pollute our mind, such as attachment and anger, are in principle separable from the mind. What this suggests is that these afflictions of the mind are in some sense adventitious. Since these pollutants are separable or removable from the mind, they cannot together constitute its essential nature. Rather, the essential nature of our mind is the potential for buddhahood which is inherent in us all.

So, as Maitreya points out, the various afflictions of our mind are separable from the mind's essential nature — whereas the potential for the perfection of enlightenment, the realisation of omniscience and the perfection of many of the enlightened qualities of buddhahood, lie naturally in the form of a seed in the very mind that we all possess. This seed or potential is referred to in the Buddhist texts as buddha nature, the essence of buddhahood. These qualities of the Buddha are not something we need to cultivate from outside ourselves but, rather, the seed or potential that exists naturally in all of us. Our task as an aspirant to buddhahood is to activate and perfect this potential for full awakening.

3

Eight Verses on Mind Training

DESPITE ALL THE MATERIAL PROGRESS IN THIS AND THE LAST century we still experience suffering, especially in relation to mental well-being. In fact, if anything, the complex way of life created by modernisation or globalisation is causing new problems and new causes of mental unrest. Under these circumstances I feel that the various religious traditions have an important role to play in helping to maintain peace and the spirit of reconciliation and dialogue, and therefore harmony and close contact between them is essential. Whether we are believers or non-believers and, within the category of the believers, whether we hold this or that belief, we must respect all the traditions. That's very important.

I always tell people in non-Buddhist countries that followers of other religions should maintain their own tradition. To change religion is not easy, and people can get into trouble as a result of confusion. So it is much safer to keep to one's own tradition, while respecting all religions. I'm Buddhist — sometimes I describe myself as a staunch Buddhist — but, at the same time, I respect and admire the works of other traditions' figures such as Jesus Christ. Basically, all the religious traditions have made an immense contribution to humanity and continue to do so, and as such are worthy of our respect and admiration.

When we contemplate the diversity of spiritual traditions on this planet we can understand that each addresses the specific needs of different human beings, because there is so much diversity in human mentality and spiritual inclination. Yet, fundamentally, all spiritual traditions perform the same function, which is to help us tame our mental state, overcome our negativities and perfect our inner potential.

In the case of Buddhism, historically diverse philosophical schools have evolved, such as the Vaibhashika, Svatantrika, Cittamatra and Madhyamika. These schools not only uphold different but often contradictory tenets, leading to vigorous debates between their proponents. Yet they all follow the same teacher, Buddha Shakyamuni, and cite authoritative scriptural sources to validate their understanding of his teachings.

To us Buddhists, what this indicates is the tremendous importance the Buddha himself placed on recognising the diversity of needs, inclinations and mental dispositions among his followers, which led him to give greater priority to their needs than to present a unified doctrinal standpoint on key issues. The lesson we must draw from this is that the essential point of spiritual teachings is their appropriateness to the needs of individual circumstances.

Historically, two main sources of scriptural lineage evolved among the followers of the Buddha's teachings in India: one was based upon the canonical texts existing in the medium of the Pali language, known as the Pali Canon, and the other existed in the medium of Sanskrit as the primary language. The great masters at Nalanda monastic university in ancient India studied and practised both of these two scriptural traditions. I believe that Tibetan Buddhism inherited and developed this rich Indian

Nalanda tradition. Prominent and highly learned Nalanda scholars were responsible for planting the seeds of Buddhism in Tibet; and especially during the period that later came to be known as the second phase of dissemination of Buddhism in Tibet, the great Nalanda master Atisha Dipamkara made tremendous contributions to Buddhism in Tibet.

What do I mean when I say that Tibetan Buddhism has inherited the Nalanda tradition? In this tradition all the key elements of the Buddha's teachings are understood in terms of two key factors. One relates to the enhancement and cultivation of wisdom or insight into the ultimate nature of reality, and the other comprises all the teachings pertaining to the cultivation of skilful means. In this context, the term 'skilful means' refers to such factors as the development of compassion, the cultivation of the altruistic aspiration to attain buddhahood for the benefit of all beings and so on — these being the spiritual practices associated primarily with conventional truth. As a preliminary to the practices of these two factors of wisdom and skilful means, we cultivate a strong sense of renunciation derived from a deep disillusionment with the concerns and activities of mundane existence.

Atisha firmly established this Nalanda tradition of

Buddhism in Tibet. Among his disciples was the Tibetan master Dromtönpa, who founded what is known as the Kadam school. This Kadam lineage was inherited by Dromtönpa's student Geshe Potowa, who in turn had two principal students, Sharawa and Langri Thangpa, the latter being the author of the *Eight Verses on Training the Mind*. This work became extremely popular in Tibet within all schools of Tibetan Buddhism as a major focus of spiritual teaching and practice. It is this short text on training the mind that we shall be reading together.

Cultivating wisdom and skilful means

In essence, the short text entitled *Eight Verses on Training the Mind* presents the practices of cultivating both conventional bodhicitta, or the altruistic aspiration to attain buddhahood for the benefit of all beings, and ultimate bodhicitta, the profound insight into the ultimate nature of reality or 'the ultimate mind of enlightenment'. The first seven stanzas present the practices related to the former while the last stanza presents the practices related to the ultimate mind of awakening.

In his classic work on the Middle Way philosophy entitled *Supplement to the Middle Way*, the Indian Buddhist master Chandrakirti compares the conventional and ultimate truths to the two wings of a bird with which it flies across the sky. In the same way, he suggests, we can traverse the vast expanse of reality by means of these two minds of awakening. The point he is making is that the ultimate aim of a Buddhist practitioner is the attainment of buddhahood, which is the embodiment of two perfections — Buddha's truth body (*dharmakaya*) and form body (*rupakaya*); and it is through the union of these minds of awakening that we can achieve this perfected state.

The real basis of dharmakaya (the Buddha's truth body) is his wisdom mind. This is described in the texts as an omniscient state of mind with the dual character of a profound insight into the ultimate nature of reality of all things, while at the same time perceiving the diversity of conventional reality in its entirety. Since that is the nature of the dharmakaya, the path leading to its attainment must share features corresponding to this ultimate objective. This path is the sustained cultivation of insight into emptiness, which enables us to transcend all the limitations of conceptual elaboration.

The second embodiment of the Buddha's enlightenment is the rupakaya or his form body, through which he assumes diverse forms in order to be of benefit to sentient beings. The path that shares features corresponding to this aspect of the Buddha's enlightenment is primarily the cultivation of bodhicitta, the altruistic intention to attain buddhahood for the benefit of the infinite number of sentient beings. This altruistic intention must be grounded upon a strong compassion that aspires to free all beings from suffering. With this altruistic intention as motivation, we engage in the practice of the six perfections.[3] The combination of these two factors of the path — skilful means, such as bodhicitta and compassion, and the wisdom aspect, which primarily entails cultivating insight into emptiness — leads to the fulfilment of our ultimate spiritual objective, namely the attainment of buddhahood.

It is crucial that these two aspects of the path are well combined, for they complement and reinforce each other. For example, deepening our understanding of emptiness has a tremendous power to enhance our natural empathetic feeling towards other fellow sentient beings and thus give rise to stronger compassion. Similarly, enhancing our compassion can expedite our accumulation of merit, which makes it easier for us to deepen our understanding of emptiness. So we can see how these two aspects of the path complement each other.

In Buddhism, when we speak of gaining deeper and

deeper levels of spiritual realisation, this also implies a correspondingly progressive overcoming of the various levels of mental obscurations or defilements. In the initial stages our spiritual practices enable us to temporarily overwhelm our negative impulses and in this way helps to reduce their force. Eventually, through sustained practice, we can totally eliminate these defilements. The process of overcoming our defilements goes in conjunction with gaining higher levels of realisation. In fact, when we speak of gaining higher levels of realisation in Buddhism we are speaking primarily of the processes through which our wisdom and insight deepen. It is actually the wisdom aspect that enables the practitioner to move from one level to the next on the path. We speak of five levels on the path: the path of accumulation, the path of preparation, the path of insight, the path of meditation and the path of no more learning.

The attainment of these levels of the path is explained in condensed form in the *Heart Sutra*, where we find the mantra TADYATHA OM GATE GATE PARAGATE PARASAMGATE BODHI SVAHA. '*Tadyatha*' means 'It is thus'; '*gate gate*' means 'go, go'; '*paragate*' means 'go beyond and transcend'; '*parasamgate*' means 'go utterly beyond, go thoroughly beyond'; and '*bodhi svaha*' means 'firmly rooted in enlightenment'.

This mantra in the *Heart Sutra* encapsulates the progression of the practitioner in terms of the five levels of the path. 'Go, go' (gate, gate) refers to the attainment of the path of accumulation and the path of preparation; 'go beyond' (paragate) refers to the attainment of the path of insight, suggesting that when one gains the path of insight — which is direct insight into emptiness — at that point one has transcended the state of ordinary existence and becomes what is known as an *arya* or 'noble being'. The metaphor of 'go beyond' suggests crossing to the shore on the other side, when one's own ordinary state is understood as this side of the shore. The other side of the shore is *nirvana* or the state of liberation. By attaining the path of insight one has already gone beyond the ordinary state of cyclic existence. The next phrase in the mantra, 'go utterly beyond' (parasamgate), implies the attainment of the path of meditation. Essentially this is a state when the direct insight one has gained has further deepened through constant familiarity and culminates in the attainment of enlightenment or total transcendence.

The point here is that this entire process of different levels of realisation, culminating in the attainment of buddhahood, is understood in the Buddhist context as a process that combines the method aspect and the wisdom aspect of the path. The entirety of the Buddha's teachings and practices is embodied in these two aspects, which are known as the two accumulations: the accumulation of merit and the accumulation of wisdom.

These two aspects can be understood in terms of how we relate to and engage in the world. For example, if our engagement with the world is at the level of diversity of things, events and objects, that is the method aspect of the path. When we engage with the world in terms of the deeper nature of reality, which is understood as the emptiness of all things and events, that practice belongs to the cultivation of wisdom.

So what is this profound understanding of emptiness that we are attempting to realise through the wisdom aspect of the path? In his *Fundamentals of the Middle Way,* Nagarjuna writes:

> Whatever is dependently originated,
> That is explained as emptiness.
> This is dependently designated
> And it is the true middle way.[4]

A true understanding of emptiness according to the Middle Way school is based on an understanding of dependent origination. In other words, dependent origination must be understood as the very ground upon which emptiness arises. Historically, two lineages of interpretation evolved with regard to understanding Nagarjuna's teaching on emptiness, one represented by Bhavaviveka and his followers and the other by Buddhapalita, Chandrakirti and their followers.

Buddhapalita explains that when we analyse things and events, particularly the world of cause and effect and the plurality of our everyday experience, we are relating to the world at the conventional level of reality. If we are unsatisfied with that level of everyday reality, however, and we go beyond it to critically enquire into the exact nature and relationship of causes and effects, analysing whether they are identical or independent of each other and so on, we are then relating to the world at the level of ultimate truth. Buddhapalita explains that when we critically subject cause and effect to that kind of penetrative questioning, we soon come to the conclusion that they are unfindable. No concepts, whether of cause and effect, origination and cessation or any others, can withstand that kind of critical analysis. Therefore, when we engage with the world, we have to do so at the level of conventional truth or everyday reality.

Similarly, in his *Supplement to the Middle Way*, Chandrakirti explains that a genuine understanding of emptiness entails a deeper appreciation of the interdependent nature of reality — that all things and events come into being as a result of dependence on other factors. Recognising this, we arrive at the conclusion that things and events are devoid of inherent existence. And as we deepen our conviction in the laws and operation of cause and effect in the realm of the conventional level of reality, we enhance our practice of the accumulation of merit. As we gradually deepen our conviction in the truth of the teachings on emptiness — particularly emptiness as the absence of inherent existence — we are able to cultivate the accumulation of wisdom. These two practices are known as the two accumulations referred to earlier.

Making a new spiritual resolve

At the level of conventional truth we all naturally possess both the desire and the potential to overcome suffering and to attain happiness. In this context, we can reflect upon the Buddha's teachings on the Four Noble Truths and the Two Truths, and on the basis of such reflection we gradually develop an understanding of how we can gain freedom from suffering and of the potential we possess within ourselves for accomplishing such a goal. We can reflect further that: 'Just like me, all other sentient beings possess this same desire and potential to be happy and overcome suffering', and ask ourselves: 'If I continue to be guided by my own self-centredness and, through my single-pointed concern for my own well-being, continue to ignore the well-being of others, what will the consequences be?'

Then we can reflect: 'From beginningless lifetimes I have harboured this self-cherishing attitude and have grasped onto the notion of an intrinsically real, enduring self. I have nurtured these two thoughts of self-cherishing and self-grasping deep in my heart as if they are twin jewels. But where has this way of being led me? By pursuing the dictates of my self-grasping and self-centredness, have I actually managed to attain the fulfilment of my self-interest? If it were possible, surely by now I should have achieved my goal. But I know that this is not the case.'

We should then compare ourselves to enlightened beings such as the Buddha Shakyamuni who achieved total victory over all defilements and perfected all qualities of goodness. We should then ask ourselves: 'How did the Buddha accomplish this?' Through contemplation we will come to recognise that, at a certain point in his existence, the Buddha reversed the normal way of thinking and being. In the place of self-cherishing he cultivated the thought of cherishing the well-being of other sentient beings, and in place of self-grasping he cultivated the wisdom realising the absence of self-existence. In this way he attained full awakening.

In his *Guide to the Bodhisattva's Way of Life*, Shantideva writes:

> What more is there to be said?
> Compare the difference between the two:
> The childish who pursue their own self interests
> And the Able One who pursues others' welfare.[5]

Through these reflections we should develop a firm resolve to cultivate a new way of thinking and being, just as the Buddha did.

> ***Verse 1***
> *With a determination to achieve the highest aim*
> *For the benefit of all sentient beings*
> *Who surpass even the wish-fulfilling gem*
> *May I hold them dear at all times.*[6]

The original version of this verse was not written as an aspiration but as a statement of resolve, so instead of

'May I hold them dear at all times' it read, 'I shall always hold them dear.' However, later this was turned into a form of aspiration. As I said earlier, normally we are concerned, in fact obsessed with our own well-being, and remain totally oblivious to the well-being of others. When we think of 'others', either we completely ignore them or we are simply not interested. At worst, we are even prepared to exploit them for the fulfilment of our own aims. The author of our text is suggesting that this is the wrong approach for spiritual practitioners. We must try to reverse this attitude so that we regard other sentient beings as precious, like wish-fulfilling jewels, and relate to them with veneration and recognition of their kindness.

The point about all sentient beings being similar to a wish-granting jewel is as follows: from the Buddhist point of view, even being reborn in the higher realms depends upon our interaction with other sentient beings. The key factor for such an achievement is the observance of the ethical discipline of refraining from the ten negative actions of body, speech and mind.[7] For example, it is impossible to maintain the ethical discipline of the first of the ten precepts of restraint — refraining from killing — without the presence of other sentient beings.

This is for the obvious reason that killing occurs when an individual takes the life of another. Therefore, the true ethical discipline of refraining from killing can only occur when an individual is presented with the opportunity to kill another yet deliberately shuns it. The same is true of all the other ethical actions, such as not telling lies, not stealing and so on, for all of which the presence of other sentient beings is essential. Moreover, many of the characteristics of our current existence, such as our physical appearance, longevity, the fact that our words carry a certain weight and that people regard them as reliable and so forth, are said to be fruits of past positive ethical actions.

Certainly, in relation to the attainment of liberation from cyclic existence, which is known also as 'definite goodness', the role of other sentient beings is indispensable. In the Buddhist understanding, the key spiritual practices that lead to the attainment of liberation are the Three Higher Trainings — higher training in morality, in meditation and in wisdom. The last two are based upon the foundation of the first, namely the training in morality. As I said before, the presence of other sentient beings is indispensable for this training. This is how we come to the powerful realisation that the role of other sentient beings is essential in all areas of our mundane and spiritual activities and aspirations.

Especially for practitioners of bodhicitta, the altruistic intention, who are known as *bodhisattvas*, it is necessary to first cultivate compassion and loving kindness towards all sentient beings. Compassion is the wish that all sentient beings may be free from suffering, while loving kindness is a state of mind which aspires that all sentient beings may enjoy happiness. So here again the focus is other sentient beings. On the basis of these two states of mind, we cultivate within ourself this most admirable and unexcelled attitude of bodhicitta. When we think along these lines, we recognise what is meant by viewing other sentient beings as though they are as precious as 'a wish-fulfilling jewel'.

In the original Tibetan version, the first stanza opens with the first person pronoun 'I' who is the one making the aspiration to work for the benefit of all sentient beings. Investigations into the nature of our personal identity and of this 'I' were major objects of philosophical enquiry in ancient India. Needless to say, our own experiences validate our personal existence. It is on the basis of the existence of this 'I' or 'self' that we posit notions of unenlightened existence and the possibility of attaining enlightenment.

The next question, then, is: 'In what sense does this self or I exist?' We all have an instinctual sense of self; we have the thought that 'I am', 'I'm doing this', 'I'm here' and so on. But if we search for the precise locus of this 'I' in our body and mind, can we really find it?

Some Indian philosophers, recognising that our mental and physical constituents — which together make up our personal existence — are transient and subject to change and decay, felt the need to posit the reality of a self that is independent of the body and mind. So they asserted that our true 'self' is an eternal principle existing independently of the body and mind, with unchanging, unitary characteristics. They felt that if the self was identified with the body and mind, this would contradict our natural intuition of our own sense of self. As Dharmakirti points out in his *Exposition of Valid Cognition*, if we were given the chance to exchange our imperfect physical body with the perfect body of a celestial being, we would be wholeheartedly willing to make that exchange. This indicates that, even in our innate intuitions about self, we do not identify ourselves entirely with our body. For if we did, this instinctive, wholehearted willingness on our part to make the exchange would not make sense.

On the whole, Buddhist schools of thought reject any notion of 'self' as an eternal principle existing independently of the body and mind. However, there are divergences of opinion among the various Buddhist schools as to the true identity of the 'self'. For example, some schools felt that the 'self' must be identified with either the physical or mental constituents of the individual. Since the continuum of the body is grosser than that of mental phenomena, various attempts were made by different schools to identify the 'self' in terms of the mental continuum or mental phenomena. One school of Buddhist thought rejects the very notion of intrinsic or inherent existence, even at the conventional level. According to this line of thought, the 'person' is understood to be a mere appellation, designation or name, and is a construct imputed on the basis of the collection of physical and mental constituents.

All of these various Buddhist schools cite a passage from the Buddha's scripture, which states:

> Just as we call something a chariot
> In dependence on the collection of its parts,
> Likewise, we conventionally label 'sentient being'
> In dependence upon the aggregates.[8]

The interpretation of this scriptural passage varies in the different schools. On one hand, some Buddhist schools felt the need to posit an intrinsic nature or objective reality to things and events, based upon the fact that our experiences appear to affirm the reality of the world in which we live and the reality of our sensations of pain and pleasure. These schools assert that although the 'self' is a construct, designated in dependence on the collection of physical or mental aggregates, when we search for the true referent of our first person pronoun 'I' we must find a basis that enjoys a greater degree of reality. They say that this basis or entity is the continuum of consciousness, which is the real referent when we use the first person pronoun 'I' and when we have the thought 'I am.' They argue, therefore, that this continuum of consciousness possesses a greater degree of reality than the concepts of 'self'. So these Buddhist thinkers interpret the Buddha's passage cited above as meaning that the existence of the 'self' must be understood on the basis of our physical and mental elements.

Other Buddhist thinkers, such as Chandrakirti, reject this notion that our first person pronoun 'I' has an objectively real referent with an intrinsic nature. They argue for an understanding of the existence of all things and events to be a mere product of conditionality — that is, their reality can only be perceived as thoroughly dependent originations arising on the basis of the aggregation of causes and conditions. To these Buddhist thinkers all of existence is a mere construct, label, name or appellation.

You may begin to wonder at this point that, if all these philosophers agree that the 'self' exists — regardless of their differing views on how it actually does — what is the point of engaging in these very complicated philosophical analyses? You may feel that, regardless of whether people believe in the inherent existence of the 'self' or not, they can still engage in the ethical practices of refraining from negative actions and engaging in positive actions. Here, in the Buddhist context, I think it is important to have some understanding of the significance of cultivating the view of emptiness. Aryadeva points out in the *Four Hundred Verses on the Middle Way* that just as the body faculty permeates all other sense faculties, such as the eyes, ears and so on, in the same way delusion underpins all afflictive emotions and thoughts. Therefore, it is only by dispelling delusion that we can undercut the arising of these afflictions of thought and emotion which cause our suffering. Similarly, in his *Entering the Middle Way*, Chandrakirti states:

With their intelligence the yogis will see that
all defects,
Such as the afflictions, arise from the egoistic
view;
They'll then recognise the self to be its object
of apprehension.
So the yogi will strive to negate this selfhood.[9]

These citations make it clear that it is our misconceived grasping onto the self and the world as possessing some kind of enduring reality which underpins all our mental and emotional disturbances that give rise to suffering. So if we truly wish to overcome suffering, we have to tackle the root of the problem somehow.

This is not something that can simply be wished for; nor is it accomplished by praying, 'May this self-grasping disappear from my mind'! Neither can it be achieved by ringing bells and beating drums or by performing impressive-looking rituals. Such a process can only be effected by cultivating true insight into the way things really are, an insight which directly opposes the way in which our fundamental ignorance misconceives reality.

In other words, we can only begin to dispel our self-grasping tendencies when we see through our deluded perception of reality. For example, if before entering this lecture hall you have formed a false belief that a dangerous elephant is in here and have therefore experienced fear and trepidation, your fears will only be removed when you see for yourself that there is no elephant in this hall. Likewise, seeing the emptiness of things and events enables us to dispel our misconception of grasping onto them — including our own self — as possessing some kind of intrinsic, independent reality.

> ***Verse 2***
> *Whenever I interact with someone*
> *May I view myself as the lowest amongst all*
> *And from the very depths of my heart*
> *Respectfully hold others as superior.*

The practices presented in this stanza directly relate to the first stanza, in which we learned to cultivate the attitude of viewing all sentient beings as more precious than a wish-granting jewel. Here the author instructs us to cultivate this attitude while maintaining a deep respect for all sentient beings. In other words, we should not have a sense of superiority, thinking that we are cultivating loving kindness and compassion towards all those other unfortunate suffering beings. Instead, we should relate to them with respect and reverence; in fact, when we interact with them, we should regard ourselves as in some ways actually inferior to them.

This relates to an important point, which is that one of the main obstacles to the practice of compassion and bodhicitta, the altruistic mind of awakening, is conceit. Any sense of conceit or self-importance gets in the way of cultivating the genuine altruistic intention, and the most effective remedy against this is the cultivation of humility. If we look at the examples of the great Kadampa masters, such as Dromtönpa, we find that their entire lives demonstrate the importance of the practice of humility. They set the ideal example of how, when relating to others, we should regard them as objects of veneration.

I can tell you a more recent story to illustrate this point. The great nineteenth-century Tibetan Dzokchen meditator Dza Patrul Rinpoche always maintained a demeanour of true humility. At one time, when he was giving a series of teachings to a large crowd of students, he experienced a forceful yearning for solitude. So one day he quietly left his residence and disappeared, dressed like an ordinary pilgrim and carrying a walking staff and very little else. When he reached a nomadic camp he sought shelter for a few days with one of the families. While he was staying with them, his hostess asked him to read some texts and, since he looked just like an ordinary pilgrim, in return for his food and lodging she asked him to help with the household chores, which included the disposal of the contents of her chamber pot.

One day, while he was away from the camp attending to this task, some of his well-dressed monk students came looking for him. When his hostess heard their description of him, she suddenly realised this was the same person she had asked to throw away the contents of her chamber pot. It is said she was so embarrassed that she just ran away! Such was the humility of this great teacher, who had many thousands of students.

Yet these great practitioners of the altruistic intention also possess a tremendous courage grounded in real inner strength. For example, Atisha's main student Dromtönpa was the epitome of humility and a very compassionate man. But he could really put his foot down and be firm, even in relation to his teacher. If Atisha happened to speak his mind rather spontaneously, Dromtönpa would not hesitate to caution him. It is even said that at one time Atisha complained to his student, saying, 'If I cannot do this and I cannot do that, why am I here in Tibet? Maybe

I should go back to India.' This combination of a total lack of conceit yet possessing great depth of courage is what is required in a true practitioner of bodhicitta, the altruistic mind of awakening.

Verse 3

In all my actions may I probe into my mind
And as soon as mental and emotional afflictions arise,
As they endanger myself and others,
May I strongly confront them and avert them.

This stanza underlines the importance of dealing with one's own mental afflictions. Although our ultimate objective is to eliminate the obscurations from our mind (especially self-grasping) that hinder us from gaining genuine insight into the way things really are, we cannot achieve this without overcoming our afflictive emotions and thoughts. Likewise, although our main objective is to help other sentient beings to tame their minds, we cannot accomplish this goal either without first taming our own mind. So this stanza shows us how to tackle our mental and emotional afflictions by applying the appropriate antidotes.

For example, when we observe our own mental processes and detect the early signs of the arising of hatred or anger, we should deliberately cultivate loving kindness and compassion in order to defuse the power of these negative thoughts. Similarly, when strong attachment begins to arise, we can counter it by deliberately cultivating practices of detachment, such as reflecting on the impurities of corporeal existence. When we detect early signs of the arising of conceit or self-importance, we can counter these by reflecting on our own shortcomings and on the Buddha's teachings on the Twelve Links of Dependent Origination and so forth.[10] Likewise, we should counteract early signs of jealousy or envy by deliberately cultivating a sense of admiration for the achievements of others and rejoicing in their successes and prosperity. This is the way to train our mind. First we observe our own internal thought processes closely, and as soon as we perceive signs of afflictions arising we apply the appropriate remedy or antidote.

The Buddhist texts describe two types of antidote. One class of antidotes comprises those that are effective in temporarily overcoming the relevant afflictions, such as the practice of loving kindness to counteract hatred, and cultivating rejoicing and admiration to counteract jealousy, as described above. The second class of antidotes consists of those that are aimed at total eradication of the afflictions, such as the cultivation of insight into emptiness that ultimately helps to eliminate the afflictions from their very root.

Verse 4

When I see beings of unpleasant character
Oppressed by strong negativity and suffering
May I hold them dear, for they are rare to find,
As if I have discovered a jewel treasure!

The expression 'beings of unpleasant character' refers to those who are ill-natured and have strong tendencies towards negative actions, while the expression 'oppressed by … suffering' refers particularly to those beings with conditions and illnesses that tend to cause them to be rejected by society. In today's world, this latter category would include people with illnesses such as AIDS. The practitioners of bodhicitta, the altruistic mind of awakening, should pay special attention towards these sentient beings and cultivate a genuine feeling of empathy for them. Instead of rejecting them, as practitioners of bodhicitta we must embrace them as if we have found a rare treasure and, on this basis, cultivate a deep sense of care and concern for them.

Verse 5

When others out of jealousy treat me wrongly
With abuse, slander and scorn
May I take upon myself the defeat
And offer to others the victory.

This stanza refers to the need on the part of practitioners of bodhicitta to cultivate a special attitude towards those who make groundless accusations against us and who pour scorn and abuse upon us. It advises that we must willingly take the defeat upon ourselves and offer victory to the other. However, it is important to understand the full context of this practice of accepting defeat and offering victory to others, including an appreciation of the special circumstances under which a different approach may be necessary.

The general principle underlying this advice is that practitioners of bodhicitta must always consider the long-term benefit of others, while at the same time considering the negative consequences of a certain course of action. For instance, rather than allowing someone to continue to indulge in unjust actions which could be detrimental to that individual in the long run, out of compassion it may sometimes be necessary to take strong measures to halt these negative acts. So accepting the defeat and offering the victory does not mean just giving in or responding with apathy. Rather, we should determine the most appropriate course of action in any given situation. The point is that practitioners of bodhicitta should not simply act out of an egoistic emotional impulse, thinking, 'If I allow him to do this, he wins and I lose and therefore I must retaliate.' This underlying principle is the subject of the following verse from Shantideva's *Guide to the Bodhisattva's Way of Life*:

> If one fails to exchange thoroughly
> One's own happiness with others' sufferings,
> Buddhahood is impossible;
> Even in cyclic existence there'll be no joy.[11]

Verse 6

When someone whom I have helped
Or in whom I have placed great hopes
Mistreats me in extremely hurtful ways
May I regard him still as my precious teacher.

According to worldly norms of human behaviour, when we help someone and place great trust in them and they mistreat us in return, it is seen as reasonable to be angry with them because we have been hurt. However, practitioners of bodhicitta must not give in to this type of conventional thinking. Instead, we should learn to view such people in a special way, as objects for our practice of forbearance and loving kindness. We must in fact recognise these people as our spiritual teachers.

> ***Verse 7***
> *In brief, may I offer benefit and joy*
> *To all my mothers, both directly and indirectly.*
> *May I quietly take upon myself*
> *All hurts and pains of my mothers.*

In essence, this stanza presents what is known as the practice of *tonglen*, which literally means 'giving and taking'. As I mentioned earlier, normally our actions are motivated by our self-cherishing attitude. Even when we engage in spiritual activities, our underlying motive often tends to be that they may be of benefit to ourselves. For example, we may engage in meditative visualisations, such as those of the Vajrayana Buddhist practices, ostensibly with the motivation to benefit others, yet there could be an underlying objective that this will bring us protection. In all our activities we retain this cherishing of the self as if it is our true refuge, our boss and our best friend, and we have the feeling that the welfare of others is totally unrelated to our own.

The practice of tonglen, of giving and taking, completely reverses this process. Through this practice we come to recognise the disadvantages of harbouring self-cherishing thoughts and the tremendous value of cherishing the well-being of other sentient beings. As we continue with the practice, over time we will come to hold this new way of thinking as a genuine treasure in our heart. This practice should be complemented in our day-to-day life by actually helping other sentient beings through such altruistic acts as giving to charity, attending to those who are sick, commiserating with those who are feeling miserable and so on.

By reversing our normal way of thinking, we try gradually to reduce the force of our attachment to self and increase the force of cherishing others' well-being. Most of the practices of tonglen are done initially at the level of imagination. Hence in the *Eight Verses on Training the Mind* we find the line of aspiration, 'May I quietly take upon myself all hurts and pains of my mothers.' The meaning of the word 'quietly' is explained in Geshe Chekawa's *Seven Points of Training the Mind*,[12] another well-known work in the genre of Tibetan mind-training texts. There is a line in this text that reads: 'Place the two astride one's breath.' This expression suggests that the two practices of 'taking' and 'giving' should be done in conjunction with the inhalation and exhalation of the breath respectively.

In the tonglen meditation, we begin with the practice of taking, which involves the visualisation of taking upon ourselves with each inhalation all the sufferings of other sentient beings, including even the origins of these sufferings and the very propensity for afflictions that exist in all beings. Then we undertake the practise of giving (which entails imagining) with each out-breath; offering our material resources, our body and our collection of wholesome karma to all other sentient beings. Our primary objective by training our mind in this way is to bring about the welfare of other sentient beings. But at the same time the fulfilment of our own interests takes place as a by-product.

When we speak of bodhicitta, the altruistic mind of awakening, we are referring to the aspiration to attain buddhahood for the benefit of all beings, which arises from a combination of two distinct but related aspirations. One is the actual aspiration to attain enlightenment, while the other is the aspiration to bring about the welfare of other sentient beings. In order to generate the first of these two aspirations, we must first develop some understanding of what is meant by enlightenment. In the Buddhist context, the term enlightenment generally refers to liberation from cyclic existence, and particularly to the highest enlightenment of buddhahood. A genuine understanding of the nature of full enlightenment occurs on the basis of a deep understanding of emptiness.

Whether or not we actually achieve the realisation of bodhicitta and to what level or depth we gain such a realisation depends upon the force of our experience of great compassion. This great compassion, which aspires to free all sentient beings from suffering, is not confined to the level of mere aspiration. It has a dimension of far greater power, which is the sense of commitment or responsibility to personally bring about this objective of fulfilling others' welfare. In order to cultivate this powerful great compassion, we need to train our mind separately in two other factors. One is to cultivate a sense of empathy with or closeness to all sentient beings, for whose sake we wish to work so that they become free from suffering. The other factor is to cultivate a deeper insight into the nature of the suffering from which we wish others to be relieved.

Traditionally, there are two main methods for cultivating the first factor, that is a sense of closeness or intimacy with all other sentient beings. One is known as the 'Seven Point Cause and Effect Method', and the other is known as the 'Method of Exchanging and Equalising of Self and Others'. It is the latter approach that is presented in the text, the *Eight Verses on Training the Mind*.

In relation to the second factor, cultivating a deeper insight into the nature of suffering from which we wish others to be freed, this will be more effective if we first train in relation to our own experience of suffering. One way to do this is to reflect deeply on the teachings on the Four Noble Truths, particularly the truth of suffering and the truth of its origin. In his *Lines of Experience*, Lama Tsong Khapa states that we will be unable to generate the genuine desire for liberation unless we deeply contemplate the nature and defects of suffering. Likewise, he continues, we will never know how to bring about the end of suffering if we fail to deeply contemplate the causal dynamics of the origin of suffering. He then makes the heartfelt aspiration, 'May I, therefore, deepen my understanding of the nature of suffering and thereby cultivate the genuine desire to attain liberation.'

As I mentioned earlier, three different levels of suffering are identified in Buddhism. The first is the suffering of suffering, the second is the suffering of change, and the third is the suffering of pervasive conditioning. As far as the first level of suffering is concerned, we all instinctively recognise these sufferings and have a natural desire to avoid them. Through deepening our understanding of this first level of suffering we cultivate the wish to take rebirth in the higher realms and, with that objective, we live a spiritual life within the framework of the ethical discipline of refraining from the ten negative actions. With regard to the second and third levels of suffering, however, we cultivate deep insight into their nature and thereby develop a genuine desire to attain liberation from cyclic existence.

When we reflect on the Buddha's teachings on the Four Noble Truths in this way, we recognise that the practice of bodhicitta really is the principal practice of all the teachings of the Buddha. We see that many other practices, such as the ethical discipline of refraining from negative actions, cultivating deeper insights into the nature of suffering and developing genuine renunciation, are in fact preliminaries to this essential practice of the cultivation of bodhicitta. Many other practices, such as the six perfections and the various meditative absorptions that one finds in the Vajrayana teachings, can all be seen as practical applications of bodhicitta. To put it in another way, we can regard these various meditative practices as precepts by which the bodhisattva must abide as a natural consequence of having generated bodhicitta, the altruistic mind of awakening.

> ***Verse 8***
> *May all this remain undefiled*
> *By the stains of the eight mundane concerns*
> *And may I, recognising all things as illusion,*
> *Devoid of clinging, be released from bondage.*

In his eighth stanza, the author presents practices related to ultimate bodhicitta, or the ultimate mind of awakening, which is the cultivation of the wisdom directly realising emptiness. He underlines the importance of ensuring that our spiritual practice does not become tainted by what are known as 'the eight mundane concerns'.[13] These eight concerns powerfully reflect the manner in which our everyday interaction with others is thoroughly defiled by our self-cherishing.

At a subtle level, even our grasping at the intrinsic existence of things is considered to be a form of mundane concern. We must ensure that all the practices of cultivating the altruistic mind of awakening remain free from any form of mundane concern, including this subtle grasping onto the inherent existence of our own self or other phenomena. This is why the cultivation of the wisdom of emptiness is crucial.

Generally speaking, there are two forms of meditation on emptiness. One is the space-like meditation on emptiness, which is characterised by the total absence or negation of inherent existence. The other is called the illusion-like meditation on emptiness. The space-like meditation must come first, because without the realisation of the total absence of inherent existence, the illusion-like perception or understanding will not occur.

For the illusion-like understanding of all phenomena to occur, there needs to be a composite of both the perception or appearance and the negation, so that when we perceive the world and engage with it we can view all things and events as resembling illusions. We will recognise that although things appear to us, they are devoid of objective, independent, intrinsic existence. This is how the illusion-like understanding arises. The author of the *Eight Verses* indicates the experiential result when he writes: 'May I, recognising all things as illusion, devoid of clinging, be released from bondage.'

When we speak of cultivating the illusion-like understanding of the nature of reality, we need to bear in mind the different interpretations of the term 'illusion-like'. The non-Buddhist Indian schools also speak of the illusion-like nature of reality, and there are different interpretations within Buddhist schools. For example, the Buddhist realist schools explain the nature of reality to be illusion-like in the sense that, although we tend to perceive things as having permanence, in reality they are changing moment by moment and it is this that gives them an illusion-like character.

In the context of our short text, the illusion-like nature of reality must be understood as relating to all things and events. Although we tend to perceive them as possessing some kind of intrinsic nature or existence, in reality they are all devoid of such reality. So there is a disparity between the way things appear to us and the way things really are. It is in this sense that things and events are said to have an illusion-like nature.

We spoke earlier about the grasping at 'self', and this has two principal forms. One is grasping at the 'self-existence of persons', while the other is grasping at the 'self-existence of phenomena', particularly the physical and mental factors of our existence. Generally, it is said that grasping at the factors of existence arises in the mind first. For example, whenever a sense of 'self' arises — such as when the thought that 'I am' is present — it does so always in relation either to our physical or mental constituents. These are known in Buddhism as the physical and mental aggregates, and grasping at their self-existence is known as the 'grasping at the self-existence of phenomena'. Based upon this delusion, the sense of self and the thought 'I am' arise, and grasping at that 'self' or 'I' is the grasping at the self-existence of the person.

Broadly speaking, there are two types of grasping at the self-existence of persons — those that focus on one's own self, and those that focus on others. The first is known as the egoistic grasping at self-existence, within which there is the grasping at the thought 'I am' or 'me' on the one hand, and the grasping at 'mine' as the possessions of that self on the other. Working from this basis we then extend the sense of self onto our belongings and so forth, such as 'my house', 'my body' and 'my mind'. Afflictions like attachment and anger arise on the basis of these possessive thoughts. This is the causal dynamic process through which our afflictions — the cause of our suffering — come into being.

In order to bring about an end to this chain of afflictive causes and effects, we need to cultivate an understanding of the two selflessnesses — 'the selflessness of the person' and the 'selflessness of phenomena'. While many texts present the selflessness of phenomena first, it is said that in terms of order of actual practice we should meditate first on the selflessness of the person. This is because it is generally easier to identify the notion of self-existence in relation to one's own sense of self than it is in relation to other phenomena.

Generating the altruistic mind of awakening: a ceremony

As a conclusion to our discussion of the *Eight Verses on Training the Mind*, let us now perform the ceremony for generating bodhicitta, the altruistic mind of awakening. Among the audience, those who are practising Buddhists can participate fully in this ceremony. Those who are not Buddhists can participate in the ceremony as a means to strengthen your commitment to the ideals of compassion and altruism.

Before you participate in the actual ceremony, as a preliminary practice you should call to mind the Seven Limb Practices — these being i) prostrations, ii) making offerings, iii) disclosure and purification of non-virtuous actions, iv) cultivating the capacity to rejoice in the positive actions of others, v) appealing to the buddhas to turn the Wheel of Dharma, vi) requesting the buddhas not to enter into nirvana, and vii) dedication.

For the actual ceremony, in the space where the *thangka* painting of the Buddha is hung you should imagine the presence of a real Buddha in person. Imagine that the Buddha is surrounded by many great spiritual masters of the past, such as Nagarjuna, Chandrakirti and Shantideva, whose works we have cited in the course of this talk. Then, with a mind untainted by afflictive emotions, reflect upon the fact that, just like you, all sentient beings have a natural desire to be happy and to overcome suffering. Also reflect upon the disadvantages of self-centredness and the self-cherishing attitude, and upon the benefits of thinking about and working for the well-being of others. Bring to mind the infinite number of sentient beings, and cultivate the strong determination that you will seek the attainment of the full enlightenment of buddhahood so that you can accomplish their welfare.

With the recitation of the first verse we are invoking the presence of all the buddhas and bodhisattvas and calling out to them to bear witness to our generation of the altruistic mind. Now, with a strong resolve and determination to bring about the welfare of all beings, arouse the altruistic mind within you.

With these preparations, let us read together the following stanzas three times:

With the wish to free all beings
I shall always go for refuge
To the Buddha, Dharma and Sangha
Until I reach full enlightenment.

Enthused by wisdom and compassion
Today in the buddhas' presence
I generate the mind for full awakening
For the benefit of all sentient beings.

As long as space remains
As long as sentient beings remain
Until then may I too remain
To dispel the miseries of the world.

We cannot expect to actually gain the realisation of the altruistic mind of awakening simply by participating in this ceremony. But if we constantly engage in the thought processes of training the mind by reciting these verses on a daily basis, and try to deepen our experience that way, we will gradually become more and more familiar with the sentiments of these verses and with the ideals of the altruistic mind of awakening. Over time we will be able to gain deeper levels of experience.

It will also be useful to remind yourself from time to time that you participated today in this ceremony of generating the altruistic mind of awakening on the basis of reading these lines. You can use this as an inspiration for your spiritual practice.

4

Atisha's *Lamp for the Path to Enlightenment*

ATISHA'S CONCISE BUT COMPREHENSIVE TEXT BRINGS TOGETHER the essential points of the teachings of all three turnings of the Wheel of Dharma, as outlined in brief in chapter two. It was composed in Tibet by the Indian master Atisha Dipamkara at the request of Jhangchup Wö, the then ruler of Western Tibet. Jhangchup Wö particularly requested a teaching that would not so much be distinguished by its profundity as by its clarity, so that it could be of benefit to the people of Tibet as a whole. Atisha was deeply touched and pleased by the sincerity of Jhangchup Wö's request, and in compliance with his appeal composed this short text.

The Indian title of the text is *Bodhipathapradipa*, which translates into Tibetan as *Byang chub gyi sgron ma* and into English as 'Lamp for the Path to Enlightenment'. The term 'bodhi' in Sanskrit means enlightenment and has the dual connotation of dispelling or clearing away something and of realising or perfecting something. It is for this reason that Tibetan translators chose to translate this important Sanskrit term with the Tibetan word *jhangchup*, which is composed of the two syllables *jhang* and *chub*. 'Jhang' means dispelling, clearing away or eliminating, while 'chub' means perfecting or realising. Together they carry the notion of the full enlightenment of buddhahood. In other words, a buddha is someone who has totally abandoned all defects and attained all positive qualities.

The path we speak of here refers to progressive stages of development of our mental continuum, beginning from the earliest spiritual realisations and culminating in the omniscient mind of the Buddha. It is referred to as a 'path' because a path is something that one travels upon; here the metaphor 'path' is used for a journey that is internal, that takes place within one's mind. Thus the 'lamp' refers to the actual teaching itself as embodied in this text. This teaching presents all the key elements of the path in their proper order. It also comprehensively defines all the essential points and explains the right sequence and how the different elements of the path relate to each other. In this sense, the text as a whole serves as a lamp to light our way on the path to enlightenment.

When we speak of enlightenment, it is generally understood in Buddhism that spiritual practitioners have different mental inclinations. Some people are more inclined to the attainment of enlightenment of a *shravaka* (listener), while others are more inclined towards the enlightenment of a *pratyekabuddha* (solitary realiser). Others are more inclined towards the bodhisattva path, culminating in the enlightenment of full buddhahood. The enlightenment referred to in this particular text is the last of these, the enlightenment of the Buddha, which is sometimes referred to as the 'great enlightenment' to distinguish it from the first two kinds of enlightenment.

Atisha's text begins with the following salutation to Manjushri: 'Homage to the bodhisattva, the youthful Manjushri.'[14] This salutation is inserted by the translator of the text from the original Indian language into the Tibetan language. There are two reasons why Tibetan translators insert a salutation at the beginning of a text. One is to ensure auspiciousness so that the task of translating the work will not face obstacles and that the endeavour will be successfully completed. More specifically, the translator's salutation is to help identify which of the three principal scriptural collections (known as the *Tripitaka*) the present work belongs to. This is in conformity with a decree issued by an early Tibetan monarch that all texts being translated from Sanskrit into Tibetan should carry such salutations from the translators. The three scriptural collections are: the collection on *Vinaya* or ethical teachings; the collection of *Sutras* or religious discourses; and the collection of *Abhidharma* or the study of Buddhist psychology and phenomenology. It was decreed that texts belonging to the Vinaya collection must be preceded by the translator's salutation to the Omniscient Buddha; texts belonging to the *Sutra* collection must have a salutation to the buddhas and bodhisattvas; and texts belonging to the Abhidharma collection must have a salutation to the Bodhisattva Manjushri. Although the *Lamp for the Path to Enlightenment* brings together the teachings of all three scriptural collections, the main theme of this work belongs to the Abhidharma collection, hence the translator's salutation to Manjushri. The Tibetan equivalent of Manjushri is *jang pel*, two syllables which mean 'gentleness' and 'glory', while the Sanskrit term 'Manjushri' is formed from the two syllables *manju* and *shri*, connoting the two aspects of the enlightened state. One aspect is the overcoming of defects, as indicated by the term 'gentleness' or '*jam*'. 'Jam' refers to the fact that Manjushri's mental continuum has been made gentle by eliminating all the afflictive forces that could make it agitated or disturbed. Freedom from those brings about the gentleness or settledness of mind. 'Glory' (pel) alludes to Manjushri's attainment of the various major and minor noble marks that define a person as a fully enlightened being. Thus, in the very name of Manjushri we see both qualities of abandonment and accomplishment or perfection.

Verse 1

I pay homage with great respect
To all the Victorious Ones of the three times,
To their teaching and those who aspire to virtue.
Urged by the good disciple Jhangchup Wö
I shall illuminate the lamp
For the path to enlightenment.

The 'Victorious Ones' mentioned in the second line are the buddhas, who are described thus because they have gained victory over the four *maras* or obstructive forces. The subtlest forms of these four forces are the ingrained propensities for afflictive emotions and thoughts that underlie the afflictions themselves; these are referred to as 'the subtle obstructions to full knowledge'. In the third line of this opening stanza Atisha pays homage to the teachings of the buddhas, which is the Dharma. Here Dharma does not refer to the literary texts but rather to the inner spiritual realisations of the Victorious Ones, or buddhas, and of the highly evolved arya or 'noble beings' who have gained direct insight into the truth.

Next Atisha makes salutation to the spiritual community, to which he applies the expression 'and those who aspire to virtue'. Here Atisha is referring to the Sangha, the community of arya beings who have achieved the path of seeing and have thus gained direct realisation of the ultimate nature of reality. In effect, in this first stanza Atisha is making salutations to the Three Jewels — the Buddha (the teacher), the Dharma (the teachings) and the Sangha (the community of practitioners).

After this verse we read, 'Urged by the good disciple Jhangchup Wö, I shall illuminate the lamp for the path to enlightenment.' As I mentioned earlier, Atisha composed this text at the specific request of the Tibetan monarch and good disciple Jhangchup Wö. This verse also alludes to a general principle in Buddhism, which is to give religious teachings to others only when asked to do so.

Understanding the Three Jewels

How can we understand the Buddha jewel, which is the first object of Atisha's salutation in this text? What are the characteristics of a buddha? To respond to these questions, it is helpful to refer to a seventh-century Indian Buddhist classic entitled *Compendium of Valid Cognitions* by Dignaga, in which he pays homage to the Buddha by giving him the epithet 'you who have become a valid being'. The operative words here are 'who have become', indicating that the Buddha was not an eternally enlightened being but someone who *became* a valid teacher by attaining enlightenment.

This demonstrates that buddhahood is not without a cause, that it does not arise from causes which are discordant with the result (buddhahood), and that the causes themselves are not permanent and immutable. So what are these causes? Dignaga identifies the cultivation of great compassion as one of the key factors. In the salutation verse of his *Compendium of Valid Cognitions*, he pays homage to the Buddha as someone who has become a valid teacher through the sustained practice of compassion, which is complemented by other practices such as cultivating the wisdom of emptiness.

Buddhist texts often refer to the Three Jewels using the metaphor of physician, medicine and nurse, which can be a helpful image. The Buddha is likened to a physician, the Dharma to medicine and the spiritual community or Sangha to a nurse. This analogy tells us that the Dharma is the true medicine that directly counters the 'illness' of our suffering and its underlying causes. The Buddha prescribes the medicine of Dharma, and our companions on the path, the members of the spiritual community, act as our support while we are 'taking the medicine' of Dharma.

The true Dharma jewel is the true cessation. The term 'cessation' here refers to the genuine freedom we gain from continuously applying the antidotes to our negative aspects of mind. So the ultimate fruit of our spiritual practice is to prevent our afflictions (our negative thoughts and emotions) from ever arising again. This ending of the afflictions is the true cessation, namely the true Dharma; and the path that leads to that true cessation is also known as the true Dharma.

So our next question would be: 'How do these antidotes work?' In this context we need to recall our earlier discussion of the three levels of suffering, when we discerned that the third level of suffering is that of pervasive conditioning. This suggests that our very existence is conditioned and is characterised by suffering. What this means is that our present existence is conditioned by karma and afflictions. As we discussed before, karma refers not only to our actions but, more importantly, to the motivation or intention behind them. The acts themselves are not the primary cause of our suffering; rather, it arises from the world of our intentions or, in other words, from our thoughts and emotions. These afflictive states of mind underlie our negative karma and are therefore the root or source of our suffering.

Obviously, these afflictions won't go away simply by saying prayers or wishing them away; they can only be eliminated by cultivating their corresponding remedies or antidotes. To understand how this process of applying the antidote works we can observe our physical world. For instance, we can contrast heat and cold: if we are suffering from the effects of too cold a temperature, then we increase the thermometer on our heater or air-conditioning unit and adjust it to our comfort. Thus, even in the physical world we can see instances where opposing forces counter each other. Another clear example is that of light and darkness. The moment we turn on a light switch the darkness is dispelled; and where there is darkness, there is no light.

In the world of our emotions and thoughts, however, the process by which antidotes work against their opposing forces is slightly different. In this case we need to develop the correct state of mind that directly opposes the particular affliction. We do this by choosing the same object but cultivating a contrary perspective or attitude. For instance, in the case of the two opposing forces of hatred and compassion, these two can be focused on a single object — such as an individual — but they will have utterly different effects in terms of our experience.

For the sake of argument, let's say a person intensely dislikes the emotion of compassion and wants to do everything possible to get rid of it within himself or herself. With this goal in mind he or she deliberately cultivates a hostile attitude towards everything, and tries extremely hard to view the disadvantages of cultivating loving kindness and so on. We can imagine how such an approach could eventually lead to an increase in that person's feelings of anger and hatred.

For spiritual practitioners, this can never be our objective. From our own personal experience we recognise that anger and hostility disturb our peace of mind and, more importantly, that they have the potential to harm others. Conversely, we recognise that positive emotions like compassion and loving kindness can engender in us a deep sense of peace and serenity, beneficial results that we can extend to others as well. This appreciation of their great value naturally leads to a desire to cultivate these positive emotions. It is through this gradual process that the antidotes work in decreasing and eventually eliminating their opposing forces in the mental realm, the realm of our thoughts and emotions.

Does this mean that there is total equality between the positive and negative emotions, and therefore that by reinforcing compassion we can eliminate hatred and vice versa? I think it is important to have a deeper understanding of the differences between positive and negative emotions. Some of our afflictions tend to be instinctual, such as attachment, anger and hostility. Although in certain circumstances there may be an immediate catalyst or trigger, and reason may play a role, generally these emotions are more reactive and instinctual. There is, however, another category of emotions that tend to be more cognitive, such as our false view of the sense of self, and grasping at certain extreme views as being supreme.

Furthermore, when we examine these afflictive thoughts and emotions we find that the subtler affliction of delusion lies at their root. Our delusory mind grasps at a substantially real existence of things, and an emotional response arises on the basis of that grasping which makes us perceive the object of this emotion as either desirable or undesirable. The mind that grasps at such things as real is deluded because the true nature of things is their emptiness — namely, that they have no independent or intrinsic existence in and of themselves. In essence, therefore, the mind that grasps at the intrinsic existence of things is fundamentally deluded. Having understood this, we come to recognise that negative emotions like anger and hatred lack any valid support, both in reality and in terms of reason, because their underlying root or basis is a distorted state of mind. Moreover, by cultivating a deep insight into emptiness, which is the true nature of things, we can undercut the very basis for the arising of these afflictions.

In contrast, positive emotions such as loving kindness and compassion tend not to be dependent upon grasping at the object as having true existence, and furthermore these positive emotions have the potential for infinite enhancement. So there are considerable differences between positive and negative emotions in terms of their basis and of their potential for infinite development.

So the question is, if delusion underlies all the afflictions, what grounds do we have for understanding this delusion to be a grasping at the true existence of things? Here we need to go back to the *Four Hundred Verses of the Middle Way* where, immediately after the verse that I cited earlier, Aryadeva writes: 'It is by gaining insight into the truth of dependent origination [that] one will bring about the cessation of delusion.' He is saying that when an individual develops deep insight into the subtle aspects of the teachings on dependent origination, he or she is then able to bring about the cessation of delusion within his or her own mind. Delusion thus is identified as a misconception, a state of mind which perceives the world and the self contrary to the principle of dependent origination.

As we saw earlier, according to this principle all things come into being in dependence upon other factors. The opposite of this would be to accord the status of independent existence to things and events; if this were so, things and events cannot have the nature of dependence upon others. This projected status of independence is referred to as 'self' in the context of the teaching on selflessness. This teaching reveals the absence of the independent existence of things, because all things come into being as a result of, or depending upon, other causes and conditions. Aryadeva concludes by saying: 'That which is dependently originated cannot possess a nature of independence, and this absence of independent existence is what I call dependent origination.'

Among Nagarjuna's disciples there was a divergence of opinion on whether or not this delusion of grasping onto things and events as possessing true existence is a defilement in the category of afflictions or the category of subtle obstructions to knowledge. On the one hand, such commentators of Nagarjuna as Parvavyeka understood the delusion of grasping at the true existence of things to be a subtle obstruction to knowledge. However, other commentators interpreted Nagarjuna's *Seventy Stanzas on the Middle Way* to mean that delusion is part of the afflicted states of mind. They argued that even to attain the state of *arhat*-hood — which is freedom from *samsara* or cyclic existence — one needs to eliminate the delusion of grasping at true existence. On the basis of that understanding, the assertion is made that the insight into emptiness is the sole path to liberation. This insight into emptiness is known as the wisdom of no-self or selflessness and is understood here in terms of what are called the Three Doors to Thorough Liberation. This insight into the emptiness of things and events is cultivated on the basis of understanding its nature both from the point of view of its causes and of its effects.

We can relate this teaching on the understanding of selflessness to the teachings on the Four Noble Truths, the first public teaching that the Buddha gave. He taught the Four Noble Truths in terms of sixteen characteristics, four in relation to each Truth. The four characteristics of the first noble truth of suffering are impermanence, unsatisfactoriness, emptiness and no-self. So all the different schools of Buddhism and all the followers of the Buddha understand that his key teaching is embodied in this teaching on no-self or anatman.

Naturally there are different interpretations of the meaning of no-self. The history of philosophical thought in India includes a very long tradition of analysis on the nature of selfhood and of the individual or being. For example, there was extensive reflection and debate around such questions as: when we experience pain and pleasure, who is the experiencer? When we speak of accumulating karma, who accumulates that karma? Who is the agent of the karmic act? Who experiences the fruits of karma? We accept the fact that there is an individual or being whom we label as 'I'; but what exactly is the nature of that 'I' or self?

Among the non-Buddhist schools in India, especially those schools which accept the idea of rebirth, there was a convergence of opinion that, since the physical body is contingent upon a particular life and is transient, the 'self' cannot be identified with the body or corporeal existence. These schools generally maintain that the self must be completely independent of the physical and psychological constituents (*skandhas* in Sanskrit) that make up an individual's existence, and posit the self as an eternal principle which transcends individual life cycles and maintains its existence throughout all temporal stages.

Whether or not the self or atman is characterised as eternal, unchanging and unitary, when we probe more deeply into its nature we can identify three principal characteristics. These are: that from the point of view of time the self is eternal; that it is unitary or indivisible; and that it is independent or in some sense self-governing. Generally speaking, all Buddhist schools reject this notion of selfhood as eternal. However, different Buddhist schools have divergent opinions as to the alternative: if there is no independent, eternal self, how do we understand the notion of a person and of the agent of action?

Who is that being? Some schools try to identify the person on the basis of the physical and mental aggregates that make up the individual, asserting that the totality of the five skandhas constitutes the person. Others maintain that one must posit the individual being or person on the basis of the continuum of consciousness. And there are others, such as the followers of the scripture of the *Yogacara* or Mind Only school, who maintain that a unique continuum of consciousness, which they call the foundational consciousness, must be identified as the person. Then there are the followers of Nagarjuna (particularly those who understand his subtlest viewpoint) who maintain that any attempt to identify the self as something independent of the body and mind is untenable. Equally untenable is the attempt to identify the self within the body and mind. They maintain that the person must be understood as a mere label, appellation or designation that is given on the basis of the aggregation of the mind and body. Thus, the nature of the person is a mere designation for something that has no intrinsic reality.

When we observe things and events more deeply, we recognise that they all come about as a result of the aggregation of many factors. None of them enjoys an independent existence; their ultimate nature is mere dependence upon other factors. However, when we perceive them more casually as we tend to do in everyday life, we form the impression that they possess some kind of discrete, independent reality of their own and we fail to perceive their interconnected, dependently originating reality. This disparity in our perception of the way things really are and the way we perceive them underpins the various afflictive and emotional responses we have in our dealings with the world.

So firstly, we can say that our distorted understanding of the world is at the root of our afflictive emotions, such as anger, hatred and attachment. Secondly, our perception of the world as having an independent reality has no valid grounding. Thirdly, when we cultivate the direct antidote, which is the wisdom of no-self, this directly counters our misconception of the world as having a true and independent existence. When we compare the two, the false view of the world lacks valid grounding in reason and experience whereas the insight into no-self has a valid grounding in both reason and experience. The viewpoint that has a valid grounding in reason and reality will become stronger as it is developed, until eventually one will be able to eliminate the false view of the world totally.

Furthermore, because the insight into the wisdom of no-self is a quality of mind its basis is very enduring, unlike a bodily quality whose basis is limited. Another characteristic of this mental quality is that once one has cultivated it to a point where it becomes spontaneous, one no longer needs to make a deliberate, conscious effort to bring it to mind. A simple catalyst or impetus can immediately evoke this understanding or mental quality.

We also need to remind ourselves that the afflictions are separable from the essential nature of mind; they are removable because their basis is a misconception, and once this has been overcome the afflictions can be removed. When we consider all of these things together, eventually we reach a point where the word 'liberation' or moksha comes to have a profound meaning and we realise that liberation is possible. We can combine that understanding with the understanding of buddha nature as explained in the *Tathagatagarbha Sutra* referred to earlier, where the essential nature of mind is described as luminous and unpolluted. We then come to realise that not only are the afflictions removable but the propensities and imprints left by these afflictions in our mind are also removable. This is how we come to conceive of the real possibility of attaining buddhahood, which is the total elimination of the afflictions and their propensities and imprints.

The state of buddhahood is described in the Mahayana scriptures in terms of the four *kayas* or the Four Embodiments of Full Enlightenment. However, a more profound and detailed understanding of the four kayas is developed on the basis of reading and studying the Vajrayana texts, in which the four kayas are presented on the basis of the subtle mind — also known as the 'fundamental innate mind of clear light'. The *svabhavakaya* is the natural embodiment of the Buddha. The omniscient mind of the Buddha in that state is described as the dharmakaya or the wisdom truth body. The subtle energy or the *prana*, which is inseparable from this Buddha's dharmakaya state and is energy in its most subtle form, is the *sambhogakaya* or 'Buddha body of perfect resource'. When that subtle energy assumes a visible form, that embodiment is described as the *nirmanakaya* or 'Buddha body of perfect emanation'. Together these four kayas comprise the fundamental innate mind of clear light, which is the state of buddhahood.

If we think in this way, we reach a deeper understanding of what is meant by Dharma. On the basis of that understanding of Dharma we can understand the Buddha, who is the example of the total perfection or realisation of the Dharma, and the Sangha, those who are on the path of realisation of the Dharma. This is how we can usefully reflect upon the first verse of this text, the verse of salutation to the Three Jewels, in order to gain a general introduction to what is meant by Dharma.

Going for refuge to the Three Jewels

As Dignaga states, a buddha is someone who has attained full enlightenment through the cultivation of compassion and the wisdom of no-self, the absence of self-existence. From our discussion we also saw how the Dharma jewel is to be understood as the path by which we can gradually accomplish the same result as the fully awakened Buddha. Likewise, the Sangha jewel is the community of sincere practitioners who have directly realised emptiness, the ultimate nature of reality.

For those of us who consider ourselves to be practising Buddhists, it is crucial to have this kind of deeper understanding of the Three Jewels when we go for refuge to the Buddha, Dharma and Sangha. For example, we go for refuge to the Buddha by cultivating a deep admiration for the historical buddhas based on profound devotion and faith in their noble spiritual attainments.

When we speak of faith in the Buddhist context, it must be understood in terms of faith that is reinforced by wisdom or intelligence. Faith must be grounded in wisdom and wisdom must be reinforced by faith and compassion, so that each strengthens and complements the other.

But we must also understand that going for refuge to the Three Jewels is related to our own inner spiritual realisations and experience of the path to enlightenment. Our faith or devotion to the Three Jewels must be that of emulation, in that we not only have admiration for them but, more importantly, we also aspire to actualise these three within ourselves. This kind of faith gives us the incentive and inspiration to engage in the practices of the path and cultivate the various levels of realisation until we attain buddhahood. Therefore it is crucial to understand that when we go for refuge to the Buddha, not only do we go for refuge to the historical Buddha but we also go for refuge to our own future buddhahood.

Levels of spiritual trainees

The actual presentation of the subject matter of the text begins from the following verse:

Verse 2

Understand there are three kinds of persons
Because of their small, middling and supreme capacities.
I shall write clearly distinguishing
Their individual characteristics.

One of the principal characteristics of Atisha's text is that it presents the essence of the entire teachings of the Buddha in a definite sequence of topics and practices, which is premised on the conviction that the effectiveness of practice is enhanced by following such a systematic approach.

We can see how this works through the example of the cultivation of bodhicitta, the altruistic mind of awakening — namely the aspiration to achieve buddhahood for the benefit of all beings. First we have to develop an understanding of the object of our aspiration, which is buddhahood or full awakening, and to do this we need some understanding of what is meant by 'awakening' or 'enlightenment'. In addition, we need to cultivate a deep sense of altruism based on great compassion, a genuine wish to see all beings free from suffering. In order to evoke such great compassion, we have to systematically develop a deep empathy and sense of connectedness with all sentient beings, a deeply felt sense that we cannot bear their suffering — as if it was our own.

Along with that, we also need to gain a deeper understanding of the nature of suffering from which we wish all other beings to be freed. As I said earlier, this entails examining our own experience of suffering so that we can develop a strong desire to gain freedom from it, which is true renunciation. When all these elements are combined we will be able to arouse bodhicitta, the altruistic mind of awakening. In order for bodhicitta to take root in us, therefore, we need to first cultivate the different components of this altruistic mind of awakening individually, and there is a certain sequence to the development of these aspects of the path. In the present text Atisha explains these various aspects of the path within the framework of practices suited to practitioners of the three capacities — the small-, middling- and supreme-capacity practitioners. He is not necessarily referring to three independent categories of individuals, some with a higher capacity, some with a middling or average capacity, and others with a small or limited capacity. What this division principally refers to is the different levels of mental capacity that a single individual may progress through on the various stages of his or her spiritual development.

Initially, therefore, individual practitioners can be said to have a small capacity. Through practice they progress to the next stage and become someone of middling capacity, and with further practice they reach the supreme capacity. We can see an analogy here with the modern educational system. Roughly speaking, these three capacities correspond to elementary school, high school and university levels, as students move through progressively higher and more specialised levels of study.

We can relate Atisha's teaching on the three capacities to Aryadeva's three phases of spiritual development as described in the following verse of his *Four Hundred Verses on the Middle Way*:

> First the unwholesome acts are averted;
> In the middle the self is averted;
> In the final all views are relinquished —
> He who knows this is wise indeed.[15]

Aryadeva uses the term 'unwholesome acts' to refer to our negative actions and thoughts, which are the main causes of our suffering. When we speak about the causes of suffering we are talking about karma or action, and a distinction is generally made between three types of karma. One is negative or unwholesome karma, another is wholesome or meritorious karma, and the third is immutable or unchangeable karma. The first, negative karma, gives rise to suffering in the lower realms;[16] the second, wholesome karma, gives rise to birth in the higher realms as a human or celestial being; and the third, immutable or unchangeable karma, gives rise to birth in the form and formless realms.[17]

Aryadeva's first stage, where the practitioner is advised to avert or eliminate unwholesome actions, corresponds to Atisha's initial scope or small-capacity stage. The principal objective here is to gain freedom from immediate experiences of suffering, and the individual practitioner's immediate spiritual quest is motivated by the fear of encountering the sufferings of the lower realms. The main spiritual practices at this stage are those of morality — refraining from the ten negative actions of body, speech and mind — and going for refuge to the Three Jewels.

The second stage in Aryadeva's three phases, where our conception of 'self' is to be dismantled, corresponds to Atisha's middling capacity. Here practitioners' primary motivation is to gain freedom from cyclic existence,[18] and the main practice is the elimination of the mental afflictions that give rise to our suffering and unenlightened existence. The third and the final stage in Aryadeva's three phases, where we relinquish all views, corresponds to Atisha's supreme capacity. Here the principal motivation is not only to gain freedom from cyclic existence but, more importantly, to also attain full enlightenment for the benefit of all beings.

One of the main points underlined by these two frameworks is that even practitioners of middling and supreme capacities must first undertake the practices associated with the small or initial capacity. Each level of practice builds upon the former and relies upon the firm foundation of the proper sequence.

The three principal factors of the path

The great Indian teacher Nagarjuna identifies three principal factors for the attainment of full enlightenment. The first factor is bodhicitta, the altruistic aspiration to attain buddhahood for the benefit of all beings. The second factor is a powerful force of compassion, which not only wishes other sentient beings to be free from suffering but also involves taking responsibility for bringing about that goal. The third principal factor is what Nagarjuna calls 'non-dual wisdom', which refers to an insight into emptiness that transcends the two extremes of absolutism and nihilism. This insight or wisdom, which understands the way things really are, is often described as 'suchness' or 'the ultimate nature of reality'.

The process or path to attaining full enlightenment is described in the Buddhist texts in terms of the 'five paths' and 'ten stages of the bodhisattva', and is said to require an accumulation of merit over a period of three innumerable aeons. Because some Vajrayana texts speak of the possibility of attaining buddhahood in a 'single instant', this may give the impression that there is some kind of special practice through which we could become fully enlightened during a single meditation session, such as simply by reciting the mantra 'HUM' or something similar. This is utterly unrealistic. Earlier we saw how our normal mental states are permeated with the pollution of the various afflictions and that these afflictions must be removed gradually, layer after layer. It is through such a gradual process that our mind becomes increasingly purified, a process that eventually culminates in the attainment of buddhahood.

Some might feel rather discouraged at this prospect, as indeed I did in my teens. I remember quite clearly making the following remark to my tutor Tadrak Rinpoche: 'Having looked at the scriptures on the bodhisattva practices, I feel the path they describe is so long that it seems almost impossible. So probably the Vajrayana path, where it is explained that it is possible to attain buddhahood in a much shorter period of time, may be more suited to me.' Tadrak Rinpoche's response was immediate. He said: 'How can there be a viable Vajrayana path without the practice of bodhicitta?'

In fact, Nagarjuna provides several arguments to help ensure that we do not become discouraged while on the path. These include the idea that if we persevere with our practice we will reach a stage of development where we will no longer be vulnerable to the sufferings of cyclic existence. Once such a stage is attained we can be quite content to remain in the world for as long as it takes to liberate all beings from suffering. Furthermore, Nagarjuna argues, since we have taken the solemn vow to work for the well-being of others, our activities will remain the same both before and after attaining full enlightenment. So the factor of time once again becomes less relevant. Nagarjuna also argues that sincere dedication to the practice of bodhicitta evokes a deep sense of fulfilment and a feeling that we are making our human existence most meaningful, which help overcome any basis for fatigue or discouragement.

To underline this last point the Kadampa masters often urge us to put all our efforts into cultivating bodhicitta, because once bodhicitta arises in us it will take care of everything. It will take care of accumulating merit for us and it will take care of purifying all our negativities. This shows us that the practice of bodhicitta is the source of the fulfilment of both our temporary and long-term aims.

Of course, if you are not interested in cultivating bodhicitta, or if you feel it is too difficult for you or that it takes too long, you are free not to undertake it. However, if you make such a choice, how are you then going to bring the continuum of your sufferings to an end? For regardless of whether we accept the notion of karma and afflictions, the fact remains that our present unenlightened existence is a product of our past karma and afflictions. And as long as we remain chained to these two, true happiness will elude us, undesirable events will befall us from time to time, and we will continue to be subject to the unavoidable sufferings of birth, illness, ageing and death.

The Kadampa master Geshe Potowa once asked: 'Is there ever a possibility of exhausting or completing our sufferings simply by experiencing them?' This, of course, is not possible. For beginningless lifetimes we have endured all the sufferings of birth, illness, ageing and death over and over again, and the passage of time has failed to bring them to an end. From this we can infer that in the future too, simply living through them over a passage of time, no matter how long, is not likely to lead to their end. Instead, we need to bring about their conclusion through a conscious and deliberate effort, and this can only be achieved on the basis of understanding the deeper nature of suffering and applying the correct means.

I would like to make a related point here. One day, when a very learned scholar or *geshe* and I were discussing the fact that the self is an elusive phenomenon, that it is unfindable in either body or mind, he remarked: 'If the self did not exist at all, in a sense that would make things very simple. There would be no experience of suffering and pain, because there would be no subject to undergo such experiences. However, that is not the case. Regardless of whether we can actually find it or not, there is an individual being who undergoes the experience of pain and pleasure, who is the subject of experiences, who perceives things and so on. Based on our own experience we do know that there is something — whatever we may call it — that makes it possible for us to undergo these experiences. We have something called discernment or the ability to perceive things.'

In fact, when we examine the experience of suffering, although some sufferings are at the sensory or bodily level, such as physical pain, even the very experience of pain is intimately connected with consciousness or mind and therefore is part of our mental world. This is what distinguishes sentient beings from other biological organisms, such as plants, trees and so on. Sentient beings have a subjective dimension, which we may choose to call experience, consciousness or the mental world.

What exactly is this mental phenomenon? Is it one hundred per cent contingent upon the body or physical phenomena? This question is not new. It was raised in ancient India where one school adopted a materialistic standpoint, arguing that mind is ultimately reducible to the physical body of the individual. Mind is identified with body, and there is no separate phenomenon apart from the body. Therefore, the consciousness ceases to exist at the time of death when the individual's body ceases to exist. They compared the mind and body to a wall and the mural upon it. For as long as the wall exists the mural is there, but when the wall is knocked down the mural vanishes. They gave another analogy of the mind and body being like wine and its alcoholic potency: when the wine is finished, the alcohol is no longer there either.

However, many other Indian philosophical traditions rejected this position. In modern times also, discussion takes place about the relationship between body and mind, and their relationship to our whole cosmological understanding of the origin of the universe. For example, according to modern cosmology, the beginning of the current world system was the event that has come to be called the Big Bang. But the question is, was that the beginning of everything? We can also ask, where does consciousness come from? One thing we can understand, both through scientific analysis and also from our own personal experience or perception, is that whatever experiences we have now are consequences of preceding conditions. Nothing comes into being without a cause. Just as everything in the material world must have a cause or condition that gives rise to it, so must all experiences in the mental world also have causes and conditions.

There are two principal categories of causation in relation to consciousness or the mental world. One is the material or substantial cause, which turns something into something else, and the other is the category of contributory conditions which make this causation possible.

The question of rebirth

The Indian Buddhist teacher master Dharmakirti points out in his *Valid Cognition* (*Pramanavartika*) that: 'Something that is not mental cannot turn into a mental phenomenon.' As we discussed earlier, something that is purely physical or material cannot become mental. Dharmakirti is referring to the fact that for an instant of consciousness to take place it must have another instant of consciousness as its preceding continuum. This is how we can trace mental causation back to the beginning of consciousness of this life, and from there we can posit the existence of a preceding life.

When I speak of 'beginningless lifetimes' or of a 'preceding life', some of you may already be wondering about this. How can I prove that successive lives do occur? Many of the ancient Indian spiritual and philosophical traditions that accept the concept of rebirth, including Buddhism, do not do so by simply making assertions with no basis. In fact, this question has been the object of a tremendous amount of reflection in the Indian philosophical tradition.

Furthermore, there is clear anecdotal evidence of children who appear to recall their past lives, some of whom come from families that don't even believe in the idea of rebirth. Naturally we need to subject such evidence to constant analysis and critical examination. When doing so, however, I think it is very important to bear in mind one important logical principle. We must be sure to distinguish between cases where we have so far failed to find something and others where we have found something to not be the case. Many phenomena that we cannot find at present may be discovered in the future, so if we are seeking to prove the non-existence of something we cannot simply state, 'This does not exist because we cannot find it.' That type of reasoning is overly simplistic.

If we do not accept the notion of the never-ending continuity of consciousness that takes rebirth again and again, many phenomena become inexplicable. We could choose to describe these as 'mysterious' or 'miraculous', but this is just shorthand for ignorance. It means, in effect, that we have no explanation for them. On the other hand, if we accept the notion of rebirth and the continuity of consciousness, we may not be able to convince everybody one hundred per cent, but at least we have a much greater explanatory resource at our disposal.

Generally, it is difficult to prove something to someone who has no experiential knowledge of it. For example, imagine trying to prove the existence of dreams to someone who claims to have no experience of dreams at all. How would you even proceed to prove that dreams do occur? Similarly, from the Buddhist point of view, although we have all experienced countless lifetimes, much of the memory connected to a particular embodied existence ceases to exist when the body changes. Since we have no ability to recall our past life experiences, it is difficult to state categorically that past lives exist. However, when highly evolved spiritual practitioners enter into deep meditative states of mind they gain access to far subtler states of mind than our normal everyday levels of consciousness. Among the meditators I have known personally, some have had quite vivid recollections of past experiences while in deep meditative states. In other words, according to the Buddhist understanding, it is the continuum of the subtle consciousness which helps connect the present state of mind to our past lives.

SCRIPTURE, *REASON AND EMPIRICAL EVIDENCE*

Having said that, if the concept of rebirth or, for that matter, any other concept adhered to by Buddhists were to be empirically disproved, given the crucial importance of reason and empirical evidence in Buddhist thought, we will have to accept the new evidence and reject our previously held concept. For example, there are numerous scriptural texts on the subject of emptiness and some of them, on the surface at least, appear to conflict with each other. So if we were to rely entirely on the authority of scripture to unravel the positions of these various texts, we would reach an impasse. The tradition in Buddhism is to look at the diversity of texts on a given subject and then employ our critical reasoning to distinguish their different levels of subtlety. We can then demonstrate the validity of taking some of them at face value while recognising that others require further interpretation.

When dealing with the everyday world, or 'conventional reality' as it is called in Buddhist texts, naturally there is bound to be a large area of commonality between Buddhist and scientific explanations. Where we find empirical evidence suggesting something to be the case, we must accept its validity because we are engaging in a common area of analysis. However, this is not to say that Buddhists believe that all phenomena can be understood simply by using our critical faculty and our ordinary mind, certainly not. Given the limits of our present cognitive ability, certain facts and phenomena may well lie outside the scope of our cognition, at least for the time being.

In Buddhism, therefore, a distinction is made between three classes of phenomena. One class of phenomena, known as 'the evident', comprises those phenomena that can be directly perceived through our senses and so on. The second is the class of 'the slightly obscured'; phenomena that we can understand through inference, using reasoning based on certain observed phenomena and through the relationship of different phenomena. The third category, known as 'the extremely obscured', refers to facts and phenomena which lie beyond our present ability to cognise. For the time being, an understanding of such phenomena can only arise on the basis of the testimony of someone who has gained direct experience of them; our acceptance of their validity has to be based initially upon this valid testimony of a third person.

I often give an analogy to illustrate this third category of phenomena. Most of us know our date of birth yet we did not acquire the knowledge of this fact first-hand. We learned it through the testimony of our parents or someone else. We accept it as a valid statement because there is no reason why our parents should lie to us about this, and also because we rely on their words as authoritative figures. Of course, sometimes there are exceptions to this rule. For example, sometimes people increase their age to qualify for retirement benefits or reduce their age when seeking employment, and so on. But generally we accept the testimony of a third person that such-and-such date is our date of birth.

Buddhists accept this third class of 'extremely obscured' phenomena on the basis of the scriptural authority of the Buddha. However, our acceptance of that authority is not a simplistic one. We don't just say, 'Oh, the Buddha was a very holy person and since he said this I believe it to be true.' There are certain underlying principles involved in the Buddhist acceptance of scripture-based authority. One of these is the principle of the four reliances, which is generally stated as follows:

> Rely on the teaching, not on the person;
> Rely on the meaning, not on the words;
> Rely on the definitive meaning, not on the provisional;
> Rely on your wisdom mind, not on your ordinary mind.

On the basis of this principle of the four reliances we subject the authority of the Buddha, or any other great teacher, to critical analysis by examining the validity of their statements in other areas, especially those that in principle lend themselves to rational enquiry and empirical observation. In addition, we must also examine the integrity of these authoritative figures to establish that they have no ulterior motive for disseminating falsehoods or making the specific claims that we are examining. It is on the basis of such a thorough assessment that we accept the authority of the third person on questions that at present lie outside the scope of our ordinary mind to comprehend.

In brief, I have been speaking about the need for the cultivation of bodhicitta as the core of our spiritual practice on the path to buddhahood, a practice which we need to pursue over successive lifetimes. To ensure that we have the optimal conditions for traversing such a path, we must be reborn in the higher realms of existence,[19] a form of existence that will enable us to continue with the practices that will eventually culminate in the attainment of the full awakening of buddhahood.

The level of initial capacity

All the essential spiritual practices related primarily to the achievement of rebirth in the higher realms belong to what Atisha calls the 'small capacity'.

Verse 3

Know that those who by whatever means
Seek for themselves no more
Than the pleasures of cyclic existence
Are persons of the least capacity.

As we discussed earlier, the principal means for attaining birth in the higher realms is the ethical discipline of refraining from the ten negative actions of body, speech and mind. These comprise three actions of the body — killing, stealing and sexual misconduct; four verbal actions — lying, divisive speech, harsh speech and frivolous speech; and three mental actions — covetousness, ill-will and harbouring wrong views. To live an ethically sound life, it helps to remind ourselves of what are known as the four reflections, namely the preciousness of human life; the inevitability of our death and the uncertainty of the time of death; the infallibility of the law of cause and effect and the workings of karma; and understanding the nature of suffering. Concerning the first reflection, some Tibetan masters have said that when we contemplate the preciousness of this human existence, we should literally cultivate the determination to make our human life something precious in itself, rather than allowing it to be wasted or to become a cause of future suffering.

Contemplating these four reflections gives us the courage to engage earnestly in the practice of the Dharma in order to free ourselves from the possibility of rebirth in the lower realms. This involves a process of training our mind, not just at the mental level but also at the level of our emotions and actions. Living an ethical life is not a case of adhering to a set of regulations imposed on us from outside, such as the laws of a country. Rather it involves voluntarily embracing a discipline on the basis of a clear recognition of its value. In essence, living a true ethical life is living a life of self-discipline. When the Buddha said that 'we are our own master, we are our own enemy', he was telling us that our destiny lies in our own hands.

Having said this, when traversing the path to enlightenment we do need to rely on our teachers as spiritual guides. In fact, it is essential that we find an authentic, qualified teacher if we are to develop a good understanding of the spiritual practices essential for leading us to full awakening. There is a Tibetan saying: 'The source of pure water must be traceable to pure snow mountains.' In the same way, it is very important to ensure that the practices we follow are authentic and are traceable through an authentic lineage of transmission.

These days there is a tendency to take bits from here and there and come up with one's own mixture. This may be fine, but if you are following a particular spiritual tradition, in our case Tibetan Buddhism, it is important to ensure the authentic source and purity of the lineage, and that your teacher is an embodiment of that pure lineage.

The level of middling capacity

In the following verse Atisha describes the characteristics of spiritual trainees of the middling capacity.

Verse 4

Those who seek peace for themselves alone,
Turning away from worldly pleasures
And avoiding destructive actions
Are said to be of middling capacity.

The phrase 'destructive actions' refers to the afflictions that, together with karma, constitute the origin of suffering. This is why practitioners at the level of middling capacity concentrate on the spiritual practices that are primarily aimed at the elimination of the afflictions. Broadly speaking, these practices fall into two categories. One is training the mind to cultivate the genuine desire to gain freedom from cyclic existence, which is often referred to as the cultivation of renunciation. The other is cultivating the path to bring about the fulfilment of that wish for renunciation. In order to train one's mind in this way, one needs to reflect upon the defects of cyclic existence and to develop an understanding of the causation chain of karma and the afflictions. Through these reflections one cultivates the wish to gain freedom and then embarks upon the path to bring about that freedom.

Briefly stated, all these practices are embodied in the framework of the understanding and practice of the Buddha's Four Noble Truths. When teaching the first truth, the truth of suffering, the Buddha identified four characteristics of existence, the first of which is impermanence.[20] Although contemplation on impermanence is also found in the spiritual practices of the initial or small capacity, the reflection is different at the level of middling capacity. At the initial capacity level, impermanence is understood in terms of the transient nature of life — that is, the inevitability of death — while trainees on the middling level meditate on impermanence in terms of momentariness, that is, the ever-changing and dynamic nature of reality. A profound understanding of this subtle impermanence leads to an understanding of the nature of suffering or unsatisfactoriness, which in turn leads to an understanding of the absence of 'self'. The interrelatedness of these subtle understandings is explained in various texts, such as Aryadeva's *Four Hundred Verses* and Dharmakirti's *Exposition of Valid Cognition* (*Pramanavartika*).

To begin with, how do we understand this subtle impermanence? When we observe phenomena around us in the natural world, whether it is a plant, a tree or even a mountain, we feel as if they do not change and they will last for a long time. But over time, in some cases thousands of years, even these seemingly enduring things change. The fact is that they are subtly changing, and we have to accept that this process of change must be operating on a moment-by-moment basis. Otherwise, if things do not go through such momentary change, there is simply no basis for the fact that we detect a perceptible change over time.

The next question is, what brings about that change? What makes something cease to exist? Do things and events require a secondary condition to bring about their cessation, or do they go through the process of cessation naturally? We can see for ourselves that things do not first come into being and then a secondary factor brings about their cessation. Actually, the very cause that brought about the thing in question is also the very cause that brings about its cessation. We could say, therefore, that all things and events come into being with the seed for their cessation inherent in them. This suggests that all things and events are under the power of their causes and conditions, and in that sense they are 'other-powered' or governed by other conditions.

In the context of our own conditioned existence, which is also subject to the same nature of subtle change, it is likewise governed by causes and conditions. The causes here refer to karma and our afflictive emotions. The root of the afflictions in particular is fundamental ignorance, which causes us to grasp at things as being inherently existent. So we can understand that our very conditioned existence is under the power of delusion, affliction and ignorance. Even the very word 'ignorance' suggests that there is something wrong with it. As long as we remain under the power of such a force, how can there ever be room for lasting goodness? By reflecting in this way, we are able to gain insight into the unsatisfactory nature of our conditioned existence, which allows us to develop a true sense of renunciation.

We can understand the statement that insight into impermanence leads to insight into suffering, and insight into suffering leads to insight into no-self, in the following way: once we realise that our very existence is under the power of the afflictive forces, such as fundamental ignorance, we also realise that it is only by generating insight into no-self — as the direct opposite of fundamental ignorance — that we will be able to eliminate this ignorance from within us. Therefore, this helps us to develop conviction in the need to generate the wisdom of no-self. Without this, we may have the impression that this whole discussion about emptiness and no-self is so complex that it is irrelevant, practically speaking.

I can tell you a story to illustrate this. One time when I was giving an exposition on Nagarjuna's *Fundamentals of the Middle Way*, which deals explicitly with the topic of emptiness, one student who did not have a prior background of learning in great treatises made a comment to another colleague. He said: 'Today's teaching was a little strange. His Holiness began with the presentation of the Buddha's path and built up the edifice one layer at a time. Then, all of a sudden, he started talking about emptiness and the absence of inherent existence, so that this whole edifice he had spent much time building was completely dismantled.' He couldn't really see the point. There is that danger. However, if we understand the importance of the need to generate wisdom into emptiness as a means of bringing about the cessation of the afflictions, particularly fundamental ignorance, then we recognise the value of deepening our realisation of emptiness. Also, as Dharmakirti points out in his *Exposition of Valid Cognition*, emotions such as loving-kindness and compassion cannot directly challenge fundamental ignorance. It is only by cultivating insight into no-self that we can directly overcome our fundamental ignorance.

This is a brief explanation of the various aspects of training the mind in cultivating a genuine wish to attain liberation from cyclic existence. The actual path or means by which we bring about that freedom is explained within the framework of the Three Higher Trainings, which I have already referred to.

The level of great capacity

Atisha continues his discussion on the three capacities by turning his attention to spiritual trainees at the highest level.

Verse 5

Those who, through their personal suffering,
Truly want to end completely
All the suffering of others
Are persons of supreme capacity.

Practitioners at this level use their deep understanding of the nature of suffering, derived from reflection on their personal experience, to recognise the fundamental equality of oneself and others insofar as the desire to overcome suffering is concerned. This then leads to the arising of a spontaneous wish to free all sentient beings from their suffering, a wish which becomes the powerful impetus for engaging in spiritual practices aimed at bringing about this altruistic objective.

The most important practice in relation to this altruistic goal is the generation of bodhicitta, the altruistic aspiration to attain buddhahood for the benefit of all beings.

Traditionally, there are two principal methods for generating such a mind. One is the seven point cause and effect method, while the other is the method of exchanging and equalising of self and others. Both of these methods help to cultivate a deep sense of connectedness and powerful empathy with others. The seven point cause and effect method relates to other beings by viewing them all as objects of deepest endearment — such as seeing them as our mothers — and then reflecting upon their great kindness. The method of exchanging and equalising of self and others goes still further, in that we learn to recognise even our enemies as a source of tremendous kindness. In addition, in this approach we reflect on the disadvantages of self-cherishing and the virtues of cherishing others' well-being.

Generating the altruistic mind of awakening

Once we have gained a deeper understanding of these methods and have engaged in their practices, Atisha advises us then to affirm our dedication to the generation of this altruistic mind formally, by participating in a ceremony of generating bodhicitta. From verse six until the end of verse eleven, Atisha describes this ceremony of generating the altruistic mind.[21]

Verse 6

For those excellent living beings,
Who desire supreme enlightenment,

I shall explain the perfect methods
Taught by the spiritual teachers.

Verse 7

Facing paintings, statues and so forth
Of the completely enlightened one,
Reliquaries and the excellent teaching,
Offer flowers, incense — whatever you have.

Verse 8

With the seven-part offering
*From the (**Prayer of**) **Noble Conduct**,*
With the thought never to turn back
Until you gain ultimate enlightenment,

Verse 9

And with strong faith in the Three Jewels,
Kneeling with one knee on the ground
And your hands pressed together,
First of all take refuge three times.

Verse 10

Next, beginning with an attitude
Of love for all living creatures,

Consider beings, excluding none,
Suffering in the three bad rebirths,
Suffering birth, death and so forth.

Verse 11

Then, since you want to free these beings
From the suffering of pain,
From suffering and the causes of suffering,
Arouse immutably the resolve
To attain enlightenment.

From the verse twelve until the end of verse eighteen, Atisha describes the great benefits and merits of generating bodhicitta, the altruistic mind of awakening.

Verse 12

The qualities of developing
Such an aspiration are
Fully explained by Maitreya
In the ***Array of Trunks Sutra****.*

Verse 13

Having learned about the infinite benefits
Of the intention to gain full enlightenment

By reading this sutra or listening to a teacher,
Arouse it repeatedly to make it steadfast.

Verse 14

The Sutra Requested by Viradatta
Fully explains the merit therein.
At this point, in summary,
I will cite just three verses.

In verse fourteen, above, Atisha provides the scriptural sources for his description of the merits gained by generating the altruistic mind of awakening.

Verse 15

If it possessed physical form,
The merit of the altruistic intention
Would completely fill the whole of space
And exceed even that.

Verse 16

If someone were to fill with jewels
As many Buddha-fields as there are grains
Of sand in the Ganges
To offer to the Protector of the World,

Verse 17

This would be surpassed by
The gift of folding one's hands
And inclining one's mind to enlightenment,
For such is limitless.

Verse 18

Having developed the aspiration for enlightenment,
Constantly enhance it through concerted effort.
To remember it in this and also in other lives,
Keep the precepts properly as explained.

In verse eighteen, above, Atisha exhorts us to dedicate ourselves wholeheartedly to the attainment of our ultimate spiritual aim, which is the achievement of buddhahood for the benefit of all beings. This, then, constitutes the full ceremony of generating bodhicitta, the altruistic mind of awakening.

THE BODHISATTVA VOWS

The description of the ceremony for generating bodhicitta is followed by an explanation of the bodhisattva vows, which Atisha presents in the following verses:

Verse 19

Without the vow of the engaged intention,
Perfect aspiration will not grow.
Make effort definitely to take it
Since you want the wish for enlightenment to grow.

Verse 20

Those who maintain any of the seven kinds
Of individual liberation vow
Have the idea [prerequisite] for
The bodhisattva vow, not others.

Verse 21

The Tathagata spoke of seven kinds
Of individual liberation vow.
The best of these is glorious pure conduct,
Said to be the vow of a fully ordained person.

Verse 22

According to the ritual described in
The chapter on discipline in the **Bodhisattva Stages**,
Take the vow from a good
And well-qualified spiritual teacher.

Verse 23

Understand that a good spiritual teacher
Is one skilled in the vow ceremony,
Who lives by the vow and has
The confidence and compassion to bestow it.

Verse 24

However, in case you try but cannot
Find such a spiritual teacher,
I shall explain another
Correct procedure for taking the vow.

Verse 25

I shall write here very clearly, as explained
In the **Ornament of Manjushri's Buddha Land Sutra**,
How, long ago, when Manjushri was Ambaraja,
He aroused the intention to become enlightened.

Verse 26

'In the presence of the protectors,
I arouse the intention to gain full enlightenment.
I invite all beings as my guests
And shall free them from cyclic existence.

Verse 27

'From this moment onwards
Until I attain enlightenment,
I shall not harbour harmful thoughts,
Anger, avarice or envy.

Verse 28

'I shall cultivate pure conduct,
Give up wrong-doing and desire
And with joy in the vow of discipline
Train myself to follow the Buddhas.

Verse 29

'I shall not be eager to reach
Enlightenment in the quickest way,
But shall stay behind till the very end,
For the sake of a single being.

Verse 30

'I shall purify limitless
Inconceivable lands
And remain in the ten directions
For all those who call my name.

Verse 31

'I shall purify all my bodily
And my verbal forms of activity.
My mental activities, too, I shall purify
And do nothing that is non-virtuous.'

This is how we formally generate bodhicitta, the altruistic mind of awakening. Following this, the trainees of great capacity must implement the ideals of this altruistic intention by engaging in the practice of the six perfections — the perfection of giving, ethical discipline, forbearance, perseverance, concentration and wisdom. Together, these six perfections comprise the essence of the bodhisattva's spiritual career. The six perfections are sometimes enumerated as ten perfections, and in this case the sixth perfection of wisdom is further divided into four: the perfection of skilful means, the perfection of power, the perfection of aspiration and the perfection of transcendental wisdom. The six perfections are also at times condensed within the three ethical disciplines of a bodhisattva, these being the ethical discipline of refraining from negative actions, the ethical discipline of engaging in positive or wholesome actions, and the ethical discipline of working for others' welfare.

Not only are these three ethical disciplines of a bodhisattva comprehensive, but there is also a definite sequence to them. In order to be effective in our engagement in the ethical discipline of working for other sentient beings, first of all we must have the ability to implement this idea in our day-to-day life. For this it is necessary to engage in the ethical discipline of gathering virtues and engaging in positive actions. However, to engage in positive actions we must first refrain from the negative actions of body, speech and mind. This is the precise order of the three ethical disciplines of a bodhisattva.

Earlier I said that the bodhisattva practitioner's aim is really to help others, which is true. But in order to do that, we must first take care of our own mental continuum. So it is not sufficient for a practitioner of bodhicitta to say, 'My only wish is to help others and work for other sentient beings', and in the process to entirely neglect the need to purify his or her own mind. That does not work.

The practice of calm abiding

From verse thirty-two onwards Atisha explains the actual practices through which a bodhisattva strives to accomplish the welfare of other sentient beings. The text begins with an exposition of the practice of calm abiding (*shamatha* in Sanskrit), which constitutes the core of the practice of the perfection of concentration. The significance of this is that if we really wish to work for the benefit of others we need to develop a certain type of sensitivity to the needs of sentient beings and, based on that, an ability to discern the appropriate level of spiritual teaching most suited to their level. Here Atisha describes a method of cultivating some form of ability to perceive others' mental states; in other words, clairvoyance or precognition. The cultivation of calm abiding is a powerful method of attaining these qualities of heightened awareness. In brief, the practice of calm abiding, especially the single-pointedness of mind encompassed by such a stable and focused mind, is indispensable for a bodhisattva's successful spiritual practice.

Bringing about a transformation of mind is something that can only take place through continuous reflection on the object of our meditation. By reflecting deeply on it and then trying to develop a profound sense of conviction grounded upon our understanding, it is possible to voluntarily embrace the discipline of the practice. This is what allows transformation to take place. We cannot expect a transformation of mind simply by imposing some kind of discipline or rule from outside ourselves. The practice of calm abiding refines our mind by developing an ability to maintain a one-pointed focus on our chosen object of meditation. When combined with the kind of analytical reasoning we discussed earlier, this can bring about the genuine transformation of mind we seek. The result is a far more supple and powerful mind than our ordinary state of mind, which is so easily distracted.

When our meditation practice is primarily focused on cultivating and maintaining single-pointedness of mind, it is 'calm abiding meditation'. However, when we choose to engage with an object for the purpose of probing deeply into its nature, our meditation becomes what is known as the practice of 'penetrative insight' (*vipassana* in Sanskrit).

Of course, we can also take emptiness as the object of both calm abiding and penetrative insight meditation, but this is really only appropriate for practitioners who have already realised emptiness. In the texts we find such expressions as 'seeking meditation by means of the philosophical view' and 'seeking the view by means of meditation'. This refers to two kinds of practitioner: those who have first gained the realisation of emptiness and then cultivate single-pointedness or calm abiding meditation focused on emptiness; and others who first cultivate calm abiding and then apply that to focus on emptiness.

Most of us would find it is very difficult to first have the realisation of emptiness and then seek calm abiding focused on it. We may feel that we have quite a deep intellectual understanding of the emptiness of inherent existence, and when we meditate upon it we may feel as if we are cultivating single-pointedness of mind focused on emptiness. But it is very difficult at the beginner's stage to ensure that our realisation of emptiness remains vibrant and stable. In the process of cultivating single-pointedness of mind, practitioners often tend to lose the vibrancy of their understanding of emptiness in the beginning stages. So, generally speaking, calm abiding is cultivated first; then we learn to apply the faculty of single-pointedness to gain penetrative insight into the true nature of the chosen object of meditation.

Atisha begins his presentation of the practice of calm abiding by explaining the need for cultivating this faculty, and then goes on to present the actual method.

Verse 32

When those observing the vow
Of the active altruistic intention have trained well
In the three forms of discipline, their respect
For these three forms of discipline grows,
Which causes purity of the body, speech and mind.

Verse 33

Therefore, through effort in the vow made
By bodhisattvas for pure, full enlightenment,
The collections for complete enlightenment
Will be thoroughly accomplished.

Verse 34

All Buddhas say the cause for the completion
Of the collections, whose nature is
Merit and exalted wisdom,
Is the development of higher perception.

Verse 35

Just as a bird with undeveloped
Wings cannot fly in the sky,
Those without the power of higher perception
Cannot work for the good of living beings.

Verse 36

The merit gained in a single day
By those who possess higher perception
Cannot be gained even in a hundred lifetimes
By one without such higher perception.

Verse 37

Those who want swiftly to complete
The collections for full enlightenment
Will accomplish higher perception
Through effort, not through laziness.

Verse 38

Without the attainment of calm abiding,
Higher perceptions will not occur.
Therefore make repeated effort
To accomplish calm abiding.

Verse 39

While the conditions for calm abiding
Are incomplete, meditative stabilisation
Will not be accomplished, even if one meditates
Strenuously for thousands of years.

Verse 40

Thus maintaining well the conditions mentioned
In the **Collection for Meditative Stabilisation Chapter**,
Place the mind on any one
Virtuous focal object.

Verse 41a

When the practitioner has gained calm abiding,
Higher perception will also be gained.

As Atisha points out, the achievement of calm abiding depends upon first gathering the right conditions for engaging in the practice. These include (among other things) seeking a place of solitude and setting aside a specific time for deliberate and prolonged practice. In terms of approach, initially it is best to undertake the practice in a number of short consecutive sessions over a sustained period of time rather than engaging in long sessions. We cannot hope to achieve single-pointedness of mind by practising meditation only once in a while, when we happen to have the time. In addition, we need to ensure that we are in an appropriate environment and, more importantly, that we have a conducive lifestyle. By this I mean that we should aim to have as few chores and concerns as possible, to maintain a sound ethical discipline, and to observe a balanced, healthy diet.

Next we need to choose a suitable object for our calm abiding meditation. We do not choose an object at the sensory level, such as a visual object, but rather an image cultivated at the level of thought or imagination. First we need to become intimately familiar with our chosen object to the point that, when necessary, we can call it to mind without having to actually look at it. For example, an image of the Buddha is an excellent object for calm abiding meditation. Choose an image of the Buddha — whether a painting or a sculpture — that is neither too large nor too small, ideally an inch or two in height. Try to imagine this image of the Buddha as brilliantly radiant and weighty as well, so that it is solidly grounded. Having conjured up this image in front of you, focus your mind single-pointedly upon it and cultivate calm abiding in this manner.

Once you have learned to call the object to mind, make a strong determination to retain the focus of your attention on this chosen object. Two elements are crucial here. One is the ability to retain your focus, and the other is the clarity and alertness of your mind. Both these elements need to be present. Without the stability that enables you to remain focused, your mind will become distracted by extraneous thoughts and objects. On the other hand, if there is no clarity or alertness in your mind, the quality of your single-pointedness will not be sharp even if your focus is good.

We must remain vigilant against the two principal obstacles to meditation — mental excitement and mental laxity. Mental excitement expresses itself in the form of various distractions and undermines our ability to maintain focus; while mental laxity undermines our ability to maintain clarity and alertness. We must therefore strive to develop the sensitivity to discern the arising of these two mental events. Our personal experience shows us that mental laxity arises when our mind becomes a little too relaxed or is downcast. To overcome this, we need to find a way of uplifting our state of mind. In contrast, when our mind is too excited or agitated we need to find a means of bringing it down to a more settled state. In other words, we are seeking to establish a balanced state of mind, one that is neither too excited nor too lax.

We can also cultivate calm abiding by focusing on our own mind as the object of meditation, as is the case in the 'great seal' (*mahamudra*) practice. To do this, it is not sufficient simply to have a definition of mind as a phenomenon that is luminous and knowing. We also need an experiential understanding of what mind is.

Here is one method that helps us achieve this understanding of the nature of mind. First, we should try to see if we can stop all memories and thoughts related to the past, and then we should try to cease all thoughts that project into the future, such as anticipation, fear, worries and so on. Once we have cleared away these thoughts entangled with past and future, we should then try to maintain an awareness of the present experience and attempt to locate the gap between thoughts. We will experience a kind of vacuum, but be aware that this is not the same as the 'emptiness' we spoke of earlier in the context of the ultimate nature of reality.

In our day-to-day experience our mind is full of concepts, even in the absence of any obvious sensory experiences. It is almost as if our mind is wrapped in layers of conceptual thought. Here we are attempting to remove these layers so that we can have an experience of the mind as it is, uncontrived and spontaneous. Through prolonged and sustained practice we can extend the experience of the gap between thoughts for longer and longer periods, until eventually we gain a true sense of what is meant by the expression 'the mind is luminous and knowing'. Once we arrive at this stage, we can choose this luminosity as the object of our meditation.

When we begin the practice of cultivating single-pointedness of mind we will realise that in our normal states of awareness we experience far more moments of distraction than of focus upon a chosen object. But with perseverance this situation will slowly reverse, so that gradually we will come to experience more moments of single-pointed focus than of distraction. And as we proceed further we will begin to refine our faculties of mindfulness and vigilance, faculties that help us overcome even subtle levels of mental excitement and laxity. Eventually we will arrive at a point where we may be able to retain our focus on a chosen object of meditation for a prolonged period of time, such as a few hours, without any distraction. This heightened state of meditative absorption leads to physical and mental pliancy, including a sense of ecstasy or bliss derived from attaining perfect pliancy of body and mind. At this point, the trainee has attained genuine calm abiding (shamatha).

The wisdom of emptiness

On the basis of the successful attainment of calm abiding, we then need to cultivate the wisdom of emptiness. In the following verses Atisha presents the practice of cultivating 'penetrative insight', which is the heart of the perfection of wisdom.

Verse 41b

But without practice of the perfection of wisdom,
The obstructions will not come to an end.

Verse 42

Thus, to eliminate all obstructions
To liberation and omniscience,
The practitioner should continually cultivate
The perfection of wisdom with skilful means.

Verse 43

Wisdom without skilful means
And skilful means, too, without wisdom
Are referred to as bondage.
Therefore do not give up either.

Verse 44

To eliminate doubts concerning
What is wisdom and what is skilful means,
I shall make clear the difference
Between skilful means and wisdom.

Verse 45

Apart from the perfection of wisdom,
All virtuous practices such as
The perfection of giving are described
As skilful means by the Victorious Ones.

Verse 46

Whoever, under the influence of familiarity
With skilful means, cultivates wisdom
Will quickly attain enlightenment —
Not just by meditating on selflessness.

As there are many types of wisdom, such as those pertaining to conventional truths, in the following verse Atisha identifies what he means by wisdom in the context of the trainee of great capacity.

Verse 47

Understanding the emptiness of inherent existence
Through realising that the aggregates, constituents
And sources are not produced
Is described as wisdom.

Atisha is not saying here that phenomena, such as the aggregates, constituents and sources, possess no origination or that they do not come into being as a result of causes and conditions. Rather, he is rejecting the notion that they possess some kind of intrinsic, independent or objective existence. When we make the assertion that certain effects follow on from certain causes, we are making such statements at the level of conventional truth — in other words, within the framework of conventional reality.

However, when we probe deeper into the ultimate nature of things, as we have discussed earlier, the very unfindability of things and events leads us to deduce that their ultimate nature is emptiness. This is what Atisha means by the wisdom understanding emptiness. We should not commit the error of thinking that there is some kind of universal emptiness, which is the ultimate nature of everything, is independent of everything, and yet exists out there on some plane in and of itself. Emptiness can only be understood in relation to things and events, including sentient beings. Our quest here is to understand whether or not things exist in the manner in which we tend to perceive them or whether, on the ultimate level, they are devoid of intrinsic reality. So our probe into emptiness and the subsequent insight we gain from it cannot be divorced from our everyday world of multiplicity and diversity. This is why Nagarjuna makes the following statement in his *Fundamentals of the Middle Way*:

> Without dependence on the conventional
> The meaning of the ultimate cannot be taught.[22]

It is crucial to fully understand the meaning of this statement. In essence, Nagarjuna is saying that we arrive at an understanding of emptiness in relation to the very things and events that have a direct bearing on our experiences of suffering and happiness.

As I mentioned earlier, many texts on emptiness state that the understanding of dependent origination is the most powerful means of arriving at the knowledge of emptiness. When, as a result of engaging in deep meditation on emptiness, we fail to find the intrinsic reality of the object of our focus, we do not conclude from this that the object in question does not exist at all. Instead, we deduce that since our critical analysis has failed to find the true, independent existence of the object, its existence or reality must be understood only as dependent origination. Therefore, a genuine understanding of emptiness must really take place. The moment we reflect upon our understanding of the emptiness of inherent existence, that very understanding will indicate that things exist. It is almost as if when we hear the word 'emptiness' we should instantly recognise its implication, which is that of existing by means of dependent origination. A genuine understanding of emptiness, therefore, is said to be that in which one understands emptiness in terms of dependent origination.

A similar point is raised by Nagarjuna in his *Precious Garland*, where he explains the emptiness or selflessness of 'person' by a process of reductive analysis. This involves exploring how the person is neither the earth element nor the water element, fire element and so on. When this reductive process fails to find something called 'person' that is independent of these various elements, and also fails to identify the person with any of these elements, Nagarjuna raises the question: where, then, is the person? He does not immediately conclude by saying, 'Therefore "person" does not exist.' Rather, he refers to the idea of dependent origination, stating that: 'The person is therefore dependent upon the aggregation of the six elements.' Thus he is not negating the fact that the 'person' does exist and is real and undergoes experiences of pain and pleasure.

From my own experience I know that I exist; I know that I have non-deluded experiences of pain and pleasure. Yet when I search for the entity called 'self' or 'I' among the various elements that together constitute my existence, I cannot find anything that appears to possess intrinsic, independent reality. This is why Nagarjuna concludes that we can understand a person's existence only in terms of the principle of dependent origination.

At this point some people may raise the following objection: isn't saying that all phenomena are devoid of inherent existence tantamount to saying that nothing exists? Nagarjuna's response is to state that by 'emptiness' we do not mean a mere nothingness; rather, by 'emptiness' we mean dependent origination. In this way Nagarjuna's teaching on emptiness transcends the extremes of absolutism and nihilism. By rejecting intrinsic, independent existence his view transcends absolutism; and by stating that things and events do exist, albeit as dependent originations, he transcends the extreme of nihilism. This transcendence of the two extremes of absolutism and nihilism represents the true Middle Way.

At this point it may be helpful to reflect a little on the different levels of meaning of the principle of dependent origination. On one level dependent origination refers to the nature of things and events as understood in terms of their dependence upon causes and conditions. On another level this dependence can be understood more in terms of mutual dependence. For example, there is a mutuality of concepts between, say, long and short, in which something is posited as 'long' in relation to something else that is 'short'. Similarly, things and events have both parts and a whole; the whole is constituted of the parts, and the parts are posited in relation to the whole.

On another level still, the principle of dependent origination relates to the subject, which is the conceptual mind that creates designations, appellations, labels and so on. As we have briefly discussed before, when we give something a label or a name we generally tend to assume that the labelled object has some kind of true, independent existence. Yet when we search for the true existence or essence of the thing in question, we always fail to find it. Our conclusion, therefore, is that while things do exist on the conventional level, they do not possess ultimate, objective reality. Rather, their existence can only be posited as a mere appellation, designation or label. According to Nagarjuna, these three levels of meaning in the principle of dependent origination pervade the entire spectrum of reality.

Verse 48

Something existent cannot be produced
Nor something non-existent, like a sky flower.
These errors are both absurd and thus
Both of the [other] two will not occur either.

In verse forty-eight Atisha is alluding to a stanza in Nagarjuna's *Seventy Stanzas on Emptiness*, in which we find a discussion of causation. In that work Nagarjuna points out that if things and events possess intrinsic existence, causation will have no role to play; this means that we cannot say that things and events come into being as a result of causes and conditions. On the other hand, Nagarjuna asserts, if they are completely non-existent it is equally meaningless to speak of their causation for they will be like a 'sky flower'. For if something does not exist, how can we speak of it coming into being?

Nagarjuna is making the simple point that when we speak of cause and effect we are speaking at the level of appearances or conventional reality. For example, when we say this son is born to that father, or these sprouts come from those seeds, we are making a simple statement that something gives rise to something else. We are not making such causal statements on the basis of searching for the ultimate reality of these things which, as we saw earlier, is emptiness.

Atisha elaborates on this important philosophical point raised by Nagarjuna in the following verses:

Verse 49

A thing is not produced from itself,
Nor from another, also not from both.
Nor causelessly either, thus it does not
Exist inherently by way of its own entity.

Verse 50

Moreover, when all phenomena are examined
As to whether they are one or many,
They are not seen to exist by way of their own entity,
And thus are ascertained as not inherently existent.

In relation to this last verse, we may question whether things and events exist as singular or plural entities and, furthermore, whether these characteristics of singularity and plurality are inherently real. If we agree that they are, we immediately run into insurmountable problems. For if things and events do possess an inherently real identity, it becomes difficult to account for the relationship we observe between cause and effect. In brief, the question is: how can we coherently understand a causal relationship between two independently real and discrete entities?

Verse 51

The reasoning of the **Seventy Stanzas on Emptiness**,
The **Treatise on the Middle Way** *and so forth*
Explain that the nature of all things
Is established as emptiness.

Verse 52

Since there are a great many passages,
I have not cited them here,

But have explained just their conclusions
For the purpose of meditation.

Verse 53

Thus, whatever is meditation
On selflessness, in that it does not observe
An inherent nature in phenomena,
Is the cultivation of wisdom.

When we have gained a deep understanding of how all phenomena are devoid of inherent existence, we then shift the focus of our analysis to the very mind that understands emptiness. At that point we discover that the mind that understands emptiness shares the same ultimate nature: it, too, is devoid of inherent existence. As Atisha explains in this text, this realisation of the emptiness of both object and subject eventually brings us to a non-conceptual understanding of emptiness.

Verse 54

Just as wisdom does not see
An inherent nature in phenomena,
Having analysed wisdom itself by reasoning,
Non-conceptually meditate upon that.

In the following verses Atisha explains why it is important to cultivate such non-conceptual wisdom.

Verse 55

The nature of this worldly existence,
Which has come from conceptualisation,
Is conceptuality. Thus the elimination of
Conceptuality is the highest state of nirvana.

Verse 56

The great ignorance of conceptuality
Makes us fall into the ocean of cyclic existence.
Resting in non-conceptual stabilisation,
Space-like non-conceptuality manifests clearly.

Verse 57

When bodhisattvas non-conceptually contemplate
This excellent teaching, they will transcend
Conceptuality, so hard to overcome,
And eventually reach the non-conceptual state.

Verse 58

Having ascertained through scripture
And through reasoning that phenomena
Are not produced nor inherently existent,
Meditate without conceptuality.

Verse 59

Having thus meditated on suchness,
Eventually, after reaching 'heat' and so forth,
The 'very joyful' and the others are attained
And, before long, the enlightened state of buddhahood.

The term 'heat' here refers to the path of preparation, a stage where a bodhisattva practitioner has reached an advanced level of realisation of emptiness, while the term 'very joyful' is the name of the first stage (*bhumi*) of the bodhisattva path.

The path of tantra

From verse sixty onwards Atisha presents a summary of the path of tantra:

Verse 60

If you wish to create with ease
The collections for enlightenment
Through activities of pacification,
Increase and so forth, gained by the power of mantra,

The four activities of pacification, increase, influence and wrathful actions are an example of the greater resources that can be found in the tantric teachings for accomplishing the well-being of other sentient beings.

Verse 61

And also through the force of the eight
And other great attainments like the 'good pot'—
If you want to practise secret mantra,
As explained in the action and performance tantras,

Verse 62

Then, to receive the preceptor initiation,
You must please an excellent spiritual teacher
Through service, valuable gifts and the like
As well as through obedience.

Verse 63

Through full bestowal of the preceptor initiation
By a spiritual teacher who is pleased,
You are purified of all wrong-doing
And become fit to gain powerful attainments.

In verse sixty-four Atisha addresses a question concerning how ordained practitioners should relate to certain aspects of Vajrayana practice, such as relying on consorts, which on the surface conflicts with the ethical codes of an ordained monk or nun. For example, he explains that trainees who are ordained members should not take the 'secret' and 'wisdom' initiations in the literal sense. Atisha explains that it is critical for such practitioners to understand the appropriateness of applying the specific aspects of the Vajrayana path to one's own situation, so that they are practised in accordance with the level of the practitioner's own inner spiritual realisations.

Verse 64

Because the ***Great Tantra of the Primordial Buddha***
Forbids it emphatically,
Those observing pure conduct should not
Take the secret and wisdom initiations.

Verse 65

If those observing the austere practice of pure conduct
Were to hold these initiations,
Their vow of austerity would be impaired
Through doing that which is proscribed.

Verse 66

This creates transgressions which are a defeat
For those observing discipline.
Since they are certain to fall to a bad rebirth,
They will never gain accomplishments.

Verse 67

There is no fault if one who has received
The preceptor initiation and has knowledge
Of suchness listens to or explains the tantras
And performs burnt offering rituals,
Or makes offering of gifts and so forth.

In verse sixty-eight the author provides the following colophon:

Verse 68

I, the Elder Dipamkarashri, having seen it
Explained in sutra and in other teachings,
Have made this concise explanation
At the request of Jhangchup Wö.

The text ends with the following statement:

This concludes the Lamp for the Path to Enlightenment *by the great master Dipamkarashrijnana. It was translated, revised and finalised by the eminent Indian abbot himself and by the great reviser, translator and fully ordained monk Geway Lodrö. This teaching was written in the Temple of Tholing in Zhang Zhung.*

With this, my presentation of the transmission of Atisha's *Lamp for the Path to Enlightenment*, with some commentaries on the key points, is concluded. I cannot make claims of having attained any profound realisations of the practices. Nevertheless, you can use what I have explained here as a key to help open more doors on the Buddhist path and, through further study and practice, to deepen your own understanding. Since many of you in the audience are members of local Buddhist centres, you can ask your teachers for a more elaborate and detailed explanation of this important Buddhist text, so that you can deepen your own understanding of the path to enlightenment.

5

Conversations with Young People

GOOD MORNING. THIS IS A GOOD TIME OF DAY FOR ME TO meet with you because, for me at least, there is great freshness both physically and mentally in the morning. In contrast, late evening is the worst time of day for me. Meeting in the morning, especially with young people like you refreshes me even further. So I am very happy to have this wonderful opportunity today to spend some time with you.

I am a Tibetan, and I come from a country which some

people call 'the roof of the world'. Geographically speaking, Tibet is quite isolated and in the past many Tibetans preferred isolation. You are Australian people, mostly white. [Audience laughs.] I think that you are in a way newcomers to this place. [Audience laughs.] So in one way, we can say that Tibetans and Australians are very different from each other. We have a very different landscape, culture, religion and way of life, but these differences are in fact minor. The important thing is that we are all human beings and, on the mental, emotional and sensory levels, we all have the same experience. From birth, we all have the right to live a happy and successful life and we also all have the potential to create such a life for ourselves. This is because we can all experience peace of mind, inner satisfaction and inner happiness. Our lives do not entirely depend on external conditions. Much depends on our own mental attitude, which we are free to develop in the way we choose. So whether rich or poor, educated or uneducated, we all have the same potential. I think it's important to reflect on this shared commonality.

Using education wisely

Time is always moving and nothing can make it stand still. Whether we waste our time or use it properly is entirely up to us. Youth is a time for study, and most of you must be fully engaged in gaining a good education. Perhaps there are some lazy students among you, like I was. When I was young, I was required to study very hard but I was also quite lazy. In fact, even today I think of myself as a somewhat lazy person. [Audience laughs.] So some of you may actually prefer being here today in this meeting to being in your classroom.

I believe that one purpose of education is to help reduce our ignorance. For example, in reality everything is interconnected. But we tend to look at things as being separate or isolated from each other, and this affects the decisions we make and the way we react to situations. If we look closely at our world we can see how interdependent we are in terms of economy, politics, the environment and society. So we should try to see our world holistically, on the basis of recognising this new reality.

Modern education does not always encourage the holistic approach, however. Instead, it favours specialisation, which often operates on the assumption that things and events are isolated or independent of each other. Specialisation is necessary, of course, and we all benefit from having people in society who are well trained and have special expertise in their particular fields. But at the same time, as a society, we must strive to maintain a wider perspective.

Education is somewhat like an instrument, which can be used constructively or destructively depending on the user. I believe that one important purpose of education is to train our hearts by instilling in us a sense of caring for and sharing with others. Another important function of education is to teach us how to maintain a sincere and honest attitude at all times. This kind of education of the heart is actually in our best interests, because we all belong to humanity. If humanity is happy, we will also be happy and receive the benefits. If humanity suffers, if the environment suffers, we will also be the losers and face the negative consequences. Human beings are social animals and so our happiness and success, and our very survival, depend on others.

Opening your inner door

People often think that practising tolerance, kindness and compassion is good for the recipient, but that when it comes to achieving our own goals we must put ourselves first. I think this is an incorrect view. In actual fact, the maximum benefit of practising warm-heartedness and compassion goes to the practitioner and not to the object of compassion.

If you only think about yourself and do not care about others, you will eventually feel a deep sense of insecurity, fear and uncertainty inside. Your inner door closes and it becomes very difficult to communicate with your fellow human beings. But if you think more about others, are friendly towards them and remain truthful and open, you will feel less insecurity, fear and doubt. Although some mischievous people may take advantage of you, generally people will respond well to your genuine feelings and your life will be much happier as a result.

If you try this experiment of opening your heart with a more compassionate attitude towards others, you will find that your inner door opens and you can communicate easily and make genuine friends. It's foolish to keep a stern, unsmiling face and still expect a friendly attitude from others. You have to take the initiative of creating a happy and friendly atmosphere. If you stay open, sincere and truthful, you will definitely receive the benefits.

So day and night, even in your dreams, try to keep a warm heart. This will bring you success and a peaceful heart and mind, and you will also attract more friends this way and they'll be genuine friends. Then, when you graduate from your studies and join society, the qualities that you have developed will make you healthier and tougher — tougher in the sense of having real inner strength.

While the various religious traditions play an important role in helping people to develop their warm heart, this does not mean that religion is an essential element. That's not the case. You can be a very sensible, nice, happy and successful person without having any religious beliefs, but you will not attain happiness and success without the good human qualities of love, compassion, a sense of brotherhood and sisterhood, tolerance, self-discipline and contentment. So whether you are a believer or a non-believer, take more care of the basic human values, of caring for one another, thinking of others' well-being, and cultivating a sense of belonging to the whole of humanity.

Learning from experience

For many years I thought of myself as young, but now I am definitely no longer a youth! However, I can still remember some of the qualities of being young, such as excitement, great enthusiasm, impatience, high expectations, and sometimes a kind of impulsiveness.

I learned a few things from my youthfulness that I would like to share with you. First, it is very important to carefully analyse a situation before making a decision and, if possible, ask others for their viewpoint rather than making decisions arrogantly or impulsively. When I was in Tibet I would sometimes discuss serious matters with some of my attendants, including the floor sweepers, who would offer some very good suggestions.

Second, try not to have too many expectations, because in reality things are not easy and we often face obstacles. Having fewer expectations means that you will be less discouraged by obstacles, and you will be able to persevere with your work or efforts towards your goal. As the Tibetan saying goes: 'Nine times failure, nine times effort.' This sort of attitude is important in life.

Then, once you have made a commitment or decision, stand firm with self-confidence. If you have already studied the situation carefully and made your decision on that basis, you can proceed with full confidence, and with optimism. I think an optimistic attitude is essential. If the problems that you encounter make you lose self-confidence and become pessimistic, then even the things you can easily achieve will seem difficult to accomplish because you have lost your inner strength. In contrast, maintaining an optimistic outlook helps you to resolve the difficulties eventually.

I think that there are two kinds of happiness. One is related to pleasurable or comfortable feelings. The other is derived from the physical or mental satisfaction we gain by successfully overcoming obstacles and difficulties. I think this second kind of happiness is the more valuable, because it brings us a deep inner satisfaction and sense of fulfilment.

Looking to the future

I would like to say again what a great opportunity it is for me to meet such a large number of young people. You are the new generation, you belong to the twenty-first century. I was born in 1935, so I belong to the twentieth century, which I describe as the century of bloodshed and violence. I think there is every indication that the twenty-first century can be more peaceful and harmonious, and that people can find a way to handle the inevitable problems more wisely and patiently, with a wider perspective.

In this context, I mention an occasion when I was

in England and I had an audience with the Queen Mother, who was ninety-six years old at that time. As she had lived through the whole of the twentieth century, I asked her opinion about whether she thought the world was becoming better or worse. Without hesitation she told me that it had improved and gave me her reasons. She said that when she was young nobody was seriously concerned about human rights violations or the rights of self-determination and religious freedom, at least not in England. But she had noticed that now people everywhere have a very strong concern and interest in these issues.

Also, if we compare our way of thinking in the two centuries, I believe that the really painful experiences we had in the twentieth century have made humanity more mature, generally speaking. This has given us the foundation to build a better, more harmonious, friendly and peaceful world. So now younger people should take this opportunity and make every attempt to create a happy world.

STUDENT: Your Holiness, what advice would you give students to help them find inner peace?

THE DALAI LAMA: Oh, that's difficult. I don't know. Maybe more holidays are one source of satisfaction or inner peace. [Applause and laughter from the audience.]

There is a saying in Tibetan that 'the learned one endures hardship while studying, but the fruits of that labour are more precious than gold.' If you think about the value of gaining knowledge for your long-term future, this gives you fresh enthusiasm to learn new things day by day. This attitude also gives you a sense of purpose and prevents boredom and weariness.

I think that a sense of competition in education is good — as long as it is the sort of competitiveness that fosters self-confidence and determination. We can have an attitude that says, 'Let us go forward' and this makes us strive to excel. But the other sort of competitiveness that engenders negative feelings towards others and a desire to stop them from winning is to be avoided, as it only creates more unhappiness and even creates enemies.

If we have too many expectations, in any field, including education and your spiritual development, this is not helpful. We often face obstacles in life. If our expectations of success are very high, the obstacles we meet will discourage us and make us lose our determination. So right from the beginning you should recognise the fact that acquiring an education takes time and effort, and that some obstacles are bound to occur. You can tell yourself: 'As long as my goal is right and my motivation is sensible, I will carry on despite any obstacles or hindrances that I encounter along the way.'

As I mentioned earlier, one of the most precious things about human beings is our combination of the brain and a warm heart. If you think more about this it will help you to gradually become a gentler and more peaceful person. Then you will easily make more friends, and day by day you will receive more smiles. And perhaps at Christmas time you may even get more presents! [Audience laughs.]

STUDENT: Your Holiness, can you please explain if there is a link between world peace and inner peace? In other words, what role does spirituality play in the bigger picture of social justice and social change?

THE DALAI LAMA: Certainly I think that world peace is very closely connected with inner peace. I believe that the way to achieve world peace is through the development of our own inner peace, starting with each individual and then gradually building peaceful families, peaceful communities and peaceful leadership. We often blame our leadership but I feel that leadership comes from society. Societies that have a very individualistic attitude and short-sighted goals are likely to have leaders who conform to and promote those attitudes. So change has to begin with individuals.

In the twentieth century there were examples of a sort of peace between nations, but I think this peace was actually the mere absence of war and violence, bred from fear of the fact that both sides possessed nuclear weapons. When I visited the border areas of central Asia, for example, I found the people there full of fear because just next door they had the Soviet army and nuclear missile stations. That's not genuine peace.

I remember visiting Moscow on one occasion in 1979. At that time the USSR was still a communist totalitarian regime, yet they described themselves as a 'peace-loving nation' — as the People's Republic of China does today. In the meantime, they were busy making preparations for war, while talking of themselves as 'peace-loving'. A correspondent in Moscow even tried to forcefully put the words 'peace-loving nation' in my mouth, but I refused to accept that. So I genuinely believe that true peace must come from within.

I think we need to separate religious institutions

from religion as spirituality. Unfortunately, some religious institutions act more like organisations or even corporations. This is not so helpful for increasing peace within communities. On the other hand, religion or spirituality is undoubtedly a source of inspiration and an effective method to increase positive human values. All the major religious traditions carry the same message of love and compassion, forgiveness, tolerance, contentment and self-discipline.

The theistic religions speak of love for God and love for our fellow human beings. Of these two kinds of love, I think the most important one is love for our fellow human beings. This is also the way to express one's love for God.

STUDENT: Your Holiness, it seems that many people are solving their problems with 'quick fixes' — solutions that only create more problems. Why do we do things that only make us feel worse?

THE DALAI LAMA: This is a very big question. I think it is almost impossible to answer in general terms. One factor, as I mentioned earlier, could be that when we face a problem we tend to just think of that issue in isolation, without considering the other factors that are involved.

Also, many of the problems we are facing today — including terrorism — have arisen because of our past negligence in certain areas. It is much easier to deal with problems early on, and much harder to solve them when they have advanced and are ready to explode. At that time they are very difficult to prevent, especially when human emotions get out of control and our powers of reasoning are lost. At that stage there is no possibility of having a meaningful dialogue.

That's what I feel. Otherwise, it's very difficult to answer your question. We have to study each case individually.

STUDENT: Your Holiness, I have two questions for you. Your struggle to free Tibet has been a long one. How do you keep up that struggle? And, more generally, how is your health?

THE DALAI LAMA: We Tibetans have our own unique cultural heritage and an ancient civilisation. When Buddhism came to Tibet and flourished there, the whole Tibetan way of life changed to a more peaceful one. So we have this peaceful culture, plus our own language and traditions and so on. Unless the Chinese Government genuinely respects and appreciates Tibetan culture and spirituality, problems will remain.

As long as Tibetans exist, the Tibetan spirit will remain. It's not just a question of one or two generations but the struggle of a whole nation. Already more than 50 years have passed since I left Tibet, yet the spirit of Tibetans inside Tibet is still very strong. In fact, in some cases it seems that the younger generation is even stronger than the previous generation. So whether I am here or not, the struggle for our basic rights will continue.

To answer your second question, I was quite ill recently, suffering from an intestinal infection. I can't pronounce that properly. [Audience laughs.] Actually, it's a strange story. My health has been very good over the past two to three years. Nevertheless, during that period some Chinese agents, perhaps deliberately, started a rumour that the Dalai Lama has cancer. Then, I became ill recently and had to cancel an important spiritual engagement in Bodh Gaya, in India, for which many people had gathered. The Chinese authorities in Tibet said: 'The Dalai Lama is just pretending to be sick in order to gain more sympathy from outside.' I was actually sick at that time. [Audience laughs.] But when I am not sick, they say the Dalai Lama has cancer.

STUDENT: Your Holiness, as an Aboriginal person in Australia, the process of reconciliation between indigenous and non-indigenous people has been very important to me. What do you think needs to be done, individually and collectively, to take the process forward? And, a related but broader question, what role do you see for young people, not just in terms of the future but also in terms of what we can contribute today?

THE DALAI LAMA: To answer the first part of the question, you need to be able to express yourselves openly and air any grievances you may have. It is important that both parties meet frequently and discuss the issues, in order to build mutual confidence and trust. Because you all live together on this continent, you need to develop a real sense of community. Then whatever legal action is necessary can be carried out in an atmosphere of warm-heartedness, with a sense of caring and community and a compassionate attitude.

Here I think it may be useful to explain that genuine compassion does not mean looking down on others and feeling pity for them. Genuine compassion is unbiased. The usual form of love and compassion that we feel for our family members and friends is mixed with attachment, and this is not genuine compassion. We need to learn to have a genuine sense of concern not only for our own relatives and close friends but also for our enemies, because our enemies are also human beings. Or at least, generally speaking, they are human beings. [Audience laughs.] Therefore, they are part of 'us', and they have an equal right to be happy.

There is a risk of misunderstanding compassion as somehow entailing disregard of our own well-being. This is a mistaken view. It is necessary for us to be compassionate towards ourselves before we can be compassionate to others. Without having the experience of genuine compassion within ourselves, we have no basis upon which to extend it to other beings.

As regards the second part of your question, every day while you are studying and acquiring knowledge and different experiences, I feel that you should also be constantly thinking about human values, such as a sense of caring for and sharing with others. I think this is very important because, as I said earlier, the brain is like an instrument which can be used constructively or destructively.

For example, the events of 11 September 2001 in the United States could not have taken place without careful, clever planning. Everything must have been carefully calculated and measured well in advance. This means that the people responsible for such a horrible act must have brilliant minds. When such minds are guided by hatred and aided by modern technology, the result is disastrous. That is why I say that while you are acquiring your education, you should take as much care of your warm heart as of your brain.

STUDENT: Your Holiness, I originally came from Bosnia and am now living in Australia. On behalf of all the people who have been through war and have experienced what it means to be a refugee, can you please tell me how it is possible to forgive?

THE DALAI LAMA: According to my beliefs, tolerance and forgiveness are related to motivation. When people hurt or harm you and cause a lot of suffering for your community, it's actually no help to feel an ongoing hatred for those trouble-makers. It just brings you more frustration and inner discomfort. Ill-feeling towards others destroys your peace of mind and eventually ruins your health.

As far as taking action to regain your rights and putting a stop to their misbehaviour is concerned, practising forgiveness does not mean abandoning your struggle. We all have a legitimate right to try to restore what has been lost or damaged. We can also have a sense of concern for our enemies' bad behaviour and future well-being. If they are engaging in pursuing the wrong goal or harmful activities and we let them carry on, they will suffer ultimately. So, out of compassion and concern for them, we should try to stop them as a form of counter-measure.

Therefore, forgiveness does not mean forgetting. We can keep the negative events in our mind and in the minds of the world's citizens and carry on our just struggle, but without any ill-feeling. Sometimes there is a danger of misunderstanding the concept of forgiveness as entailing submission or giving in to one's antagonist, but this is mistaken. The proper meaning of forgiveness is not to harbour ill-will.

STUDENT: Your Holiness, in my involvement with suicide prevention programmes I have met a lot of young people who feel they have nothing to live for. As someone who always comes across as being so happy and full of joy, what would you say to those people?

THE DALAI LAMA: This is rather complicated, because each case is different. Sometimes people are too impatient; their expectations are very high and they are not prepared for difficulties. When problems arise, as they are bound to in life, the situation seems unbearable and they choose death rather than life.

Children who have grown up in a loving family atmosphere tend to be much healthier than those who live alone or, even worse, are beaten and abused and never shown genuine love. There's more danger with the latter cases that they will become violent inside and perform violent acts in society. Suicide is a form of violence, because nobody would commit suicide if they felt happy.

So I think that family is very important, including the quality of the parents' marriage. A happy, lasting marriage, built not just on physical attraction but on mutual respect, enables conflicts within the family to be resolved. Children brought up in that kind of family usually receive a better kind of affection. If the marriage does not have such a foundation, the parents may be constantly fighting and may find it difficult to show affection to their children. Many of these factors are interconnected.

It is important to take a long-term view, especially in modern times when many material facilities and services give quick results. Automatic machines are useful, of course, but human beings are not automatic; we can't simply flick a switch.

If we try to adapt that automation to our lives and expect fast results every time, this will lead to disappointment or worse.

STUDENT: What can we, as students, do to help the people of Tibet?

THE DALAI LAMA: I think the first thing you can do is to educate yourselves about Tibetan culture and the Tibetan environment — these two things are my main concern. The preservation of Tibetan culture is not only in the interests of the six million Tibetan people, but also in the interests of at least 13 or 14 million people in the northern Himalayan regions who follow the Tibetan Buddhist tradition. These people include Indians, Bhutanese, Nepalis, Mongolians, people living in some of the republics in the Russian Federation, and the Chinese. For example, traditionally China was a Buddhist country. Even today, despite difficult circumstances, more and more Chinese people are showing a genuine interest in Tibetan Buddhism. Also, to some extent I feel that Tibetan Buddhist culture can make a contribution to the peace of mind of humanity as a whole.

Then, geographically speaking, the source of all the major rivers that sustain Pakistan, India, the former Indo-Chinese region and China lies in Tibet. So if the environmental situation in Tibet changes dramatically as a result of deforestation and indiscriminate mining, the lives of millions of people are affected for the worse.

Therefore, irrespective of Tibet's political status, it is very important to preserve and protect Tibetan culture and the Tibetan environment. This is why I would like to encourage you to find out more and become well-informed on these topics. Perhaps you can then establish some student support groups for Tibet, as they have done in America, and use these groups as a forum for discussion on these issues. In this way, you can educate each other and also take the discussion out to the wider community.

STUDENT: How did you become the Dalai Lama?

THE DALAI LAMA: Some people call me 'living Buddha' or 'god-king' but these are nonsense. I am just another human being, and I usually describe myself as a simple Buddhist monk. As long as people recognise me as the Dalai Lama, I am the Dalai Lama. When they cease to recognise me, then I am not the Dalai Lama. But as long as I continue to keep my precepts as a Buddhist monk, nobody can change that. During the Cultural Revolution, Chinese propaganda called me a 'ghost' or 'the wolf in monk's robes'. But still I remain here as a Buddhist monk, so there's no change.

STUDENT: You inspire plenty of people and make people feel at ease. What gives you inspiration?

THE DALAI LAMA: Basically, I'm a Buddhist monk and Buddhist practitioner. Not necessarily a very serious practitioner, but I certainly consider myself to be a practitioner and one of my main practices is altruism. I received the Nobel Peace Prize in 1989, but my work for peace through the skilful means of compassion, altruism and non-violence is part of my spiritual practice. So, as I told them after the Peace Prize was announced, I shall remain a simple Buddhist monk, no more, no less.

Also, the Buddha's own teachings and the commentaries upon them by many great Indian masters have helped to shape my mind to be more compassionate, which gives me inner strength and widens my perspective. As a result, problems don't cause my mind much disturbance. So these teachings are a constant source of inspiration for me.

Another factor is that whoever I meet I always consider them as just another human being. I don't care what their background is — whether they are educated or uneducated, rich or poor, whether they have this or that rank — as long as they have a smile on their face and are sincere, which I can see in their eyes, I feel very happy. I think that my own calm and friendly attitude brings a similar response from them, and their response gives me another sort of strength.

Lastly, the Buddha said that we are our own master. Accordingly, I care for myself compassionately and treat all other beings as just like a part of myself. I consider this to be a meaningful perspective and a meaningful life, day by day, week by week, month by month and year by year. You also have the same potential. You should think with self-confidence that you hold your future in your own hands.

Everybody here in this hall, however young and healthy, has to die one day. I am now sixty-seven years old, so I think my death may come a little sooner than some of you, but sooner or later we all have to die. If on that last day, with your last breath, you can look back on your whole life and feel that it has been meaningful, that you have done some good things for others or at least not harmed them, then I think you can die feeling happy.

6
The Oneness of Humanity

First of all, I would like to thank those individuals and organisations who have been involved in making this event possible. I would also like to express my deep appreciation to former Prime Minister David Lange for introducing me today. We have only known each other since my second trip to this country, but before that I had heard about his strenuous efforts against nuclear weaponry. As I try to promote the message of peace and non-violence worldwide, so that we can strive towards an eventual goal of global demilitarisation, I have always admired Prime Minister Lange's courage and his political will. Some leaders find it difficult to carry through certain decisions, but I think he has shown consistent political will and determination on this issue. So, on my third visit to New Zealand, I am very happy to meet Mr Lange again.

The benefits of warm-heartedness

I started this trip to Australia and New Zealand about two weeks ago, and tomorrow morning I return to India. The very nature of time is such that it is always moving. No force can control it or make it stand still. What is important is whether or not we use time properly. I don't mean just passing the day, or going for more holidays or picnics or to nightclubs. I mean using time, if possible, to help each other and share each other's problems. If not, then at least we should refrain from harming others. By living our life in such a responsible manner we can make it meaningful.

Generally, the maximum lifespan of a human being is around 100 years, and our very existence on this planet is not intended to create pain for others. If we share our life and happiness with other people with a big smile, a warm heart and friendship, I think that is the proper way to fulfil the purpose of our existence. Creating pain and discomfort for others eventually causes pain and discomfort within ourselves, so helping others is actually the best way to achieve a deep sense of inner satisfaction.

I have nothing special to tell you here other than to share my own personal experience, which has shown me that living as a more warm-hearted person is the real basis for happiness. So I would like to encourage you to think more about inner spiritual values and learn to be warm-hearted. There are many benefits to appreciating our inner spiritual values. First, everyone is concerned about their health. Warm-heartedness makes the physical elements of the body more balanced by reducing fear and anxiety. This helps us to develop self-confidence and a sense of security, which also creates more balance in our physical body.

When my friends see that my physical health is very good they often ask me what my secret is. I tell them, 'There is no secret, nothing special.' Generally, my daily routine may be more calm and regular than most, so that could be one factor. But a more important factor seems to be my mental state, which remains quite calm in spite of some difficulties, tragic events or even my own illness or pain.

We have a saying about how to receive tragic news: 'If some unwanted or unhappy news is coming in one ear, then let it go out from the other ear.' In other words, we try not to let it remain inside our head where it will only cause more worry. In my own case, when an unhappy experience or thought arises in my mind like a wave, underneath it — like the stable ocean beneath — my principal mind basically remains quite calm. I think that could be one factor contributing to my good health. Having said that, you may have noticed that there are now a few white strands of hair in my eyebrows, which have appeared over the last five years. So with age some changes are happening in my body.

Working with our daily difficulties

A calm mind is a very positive factor. Your doctor may tell you to get more rest, but 'rest' in this sense simply refers to lying down. However, a mind that is full of worry and agitation will never give you true rest. Genuine rest is mental rest. In fact, this is more important than physical rest.

One natural fact of life is that we are always going to face some problems. It's a mistake to look for their solutions only from outside. In terms of social and political issues, of course, we can and should seek help from various sources. However, when dealing with many of life's inevitable problems we must not ignore our inner resources as well.

For example, if we look at a problem close up it appears enormous and almost insurmountable, whereas if we look at the same problem from a wider perspective it does not feel so significant or unbearable. This wider perspective gives us the necessary courage to deal with it. Say, for example, we lose a loved one or something very precious to us. Our grief only increases by being absorbed in our loss, and can reach a dangerous point where it becomes unbearable and begins to paralyse us. The situation is very different if we are able to think along the following lines: 'I'm not the only one experiencing this kind of loss; many others are going through a similar tragedy. But, in my case, at least I have lots of people helping me.' Responding to tragic events in this manner really helps us come to terms with our loss.

I lost my country when I was young and have been a refugee for more than 43 years. So I have spent most of my life away from home. From one viewpoint this is a cause of worry and inner discomfort. But from another angle I can see how this tragedy has brought me more opportunities for meeting with people from all walks of life. Also, by being a refugee, it has helped the person who carries the title 'the Dalai Lama' to be closer to reality. In Tibet, the position of the Dalai Lama sometimes seemed restricted by too much formality and ceremony; now, in exile, these restrictions have gone. So in one way it is sad, but in another way it has opened up new opportunities.

Frankly speaking, we must accept the facts of illness, old age and death. If we see these as part of life, we feel more at ease in our mind when unwanted events befall us. On the other hand, if we refuse to accept these things and think of them as almost inconceivable, it becomes much more difficult to deal with them when they actually occur. Furthermore, as everything is relative we can always find a different perspective on a given situation, no matter how tragic and unbearable it may seem.

The lesson here is not to worry too much. For those of religious faith, there are additional resources upon which to draw. For example, when Buddhists such as myself experience tragic situations we often attribute the event to our own past karma, which is helpful in coping with the tragedy. Although the actual tragedy is the same our attitude makes a substantial difference.

This is why I suggest that when you encounter problems and difficulties in your daily life, you should think about them as objectively as you can and try to look at them from different angles. This may help you perceive something positive in them.

Another important factor is self-confidence. To develop this we should be honest and sincere and, as much as possible, free from deception and pretension. If I try to pretend that I am a holy person and that I have something special to offer you, this will only cause me more worry and uneasiness. Instead, I gain self-confidence and inner strength from remaining straightforward and completely informal. Self-confidence enables us to overcome even serious problems and helps develop a stronger will and determination.

Our human family

These days there is a genuine desire for peace and a genuine concern about the environment, and each of us has the responsibility of making a contribution to these important global issues. In this respect I feel that fostering a sense of the oneness of humanity is crucial. Certainly, given the world's diverse religious traditions, ethnicities, cultural and language groups, our human family is composed of many different members. But I feel these differences are secondary to the fact that we are all members of one and the same family.

This recognition of the oneness of humanity is particularly important in the present world, which has been made smaller by technology, population growth and global economies. As a result, taking care of others' welfare has actually become a source of immense benefit to ourselves. The new reality of our world is that the destruction of our neighbour is essentially the destruction of ourselves. Every part of the world has effectively become a part of ourselves.

Differences of religious faith, social background, education and race are secondary to the basic and simple fact that we are all, each of us, the same human beings mentally, emotionally and physically. I believe that reflecting more on our 'oneness' will enable us to solve many of the problems that we face today at the global level.

The twentieth century taught us that the atomic bomb and other weapons capable of mass destruction have not solved all our problems but have in fact created others, including damage to ecology and the spread of a deeper fear and anxiety. It is true that the so-called 'mutually assured destruction' policy of deterrence in relation to nuclear weaponry appeared to bring peace, at least in Europe, during a period of great anxiety in the last century. But if we examine this situation closely, we learn that the peace in Europe was not genuine peace but the mere absence of war based on fear.

The twentieth century effectively became one of bloodshed. I think people everywhere are now frankly getting fed up with violence, not just the violence between nations but also within communities. Sometimes we even hear of violence among children in the classroom, which is really unfortunate. I think this is a powerful symptom of some terrible lack in society. I have participated in several seminars on the subject of youth unrest, alongside psychologists, social theorists, social workers, doctors, therapists and others. They unanimously agree that one factor behind today's unrest among the youth is a general lack of human affection, both in families and in society as a whole. This shows us that it is in our own interests to try to create a more affectionate human society.

So, learning from our painful experiences of the twentieth century, we should all put effort into making this twenty-first century less violent and destructive. For this we need an effective method to combat conflict other than through counter-violence, and I feel that this method is dialogue in the spirit of reconciliation. While we are promoting peace, we must also promote the spirit of dialogue. In brief, we should all strive to make this new century a century of peace and dialogue. I often suggest that school curricula should include a subject on dialogue and the peaceful resolution of conflict, so that from a young age children can learn to respond automatically to conflict in that spirit rather than through using force. I think that using force is an uncivilised and outdated method of resolving conflicts.

An important issue related to this old way of resolving conflict through violence is the continued discrimination based on gender difference. In olden times a big and strong body was seen as superior, based on the fact that the male body is usually stronger and the female a little weaker. It seems that our current attitude to male and female bears traces of this ancient way of thinking, even though in today's world the brain and our warm heart have become much more important than physical size. So this fundamental transformation in our consciousness should be reflected in our view of the world and our way of dealing with problems.

Whenever I have the opportunity I try to share these

thoughts with others, so that we can all strive to build a healthier and happier world together. After all, the responsibility for the future of our world lies entirely on the shoulders of all of us. Tomorrow I will be on my way back to India where I live. I would like to request that you think about some of the points I have raised tonight and, if they are of interest to you and if you find reflecting on them worthwhile, please try to implement them in your personal life. For example, people in relationships often fight. I suggest that from now on you smile more, try to listen to your partner and to minimise your anger and harsh words.

On the other hand, if some of you feel that my talk is only empty words and that there is not much substance, you can simply forget what I have said. That's fine, too!

Thank you very much.

QUESTION: What is your response to the fear of terrorism?

THE DALAI LAMA: With regard to the question of immediate counter-measures or response to terrorist activity, I do not know. The world leaders, led by the President of the United States, have taken some kind of worldwide initiative. Whether it's sometimes better to use force or not is difficult to say. I believe that some of these tragic situations are symptomatic of our past negligence. I think the key factors of our ultimate response should be the promotion of basic human values and seeking a peaceful resolution. It is far better to meet one's opponents in a spirit of dialogue, honesty and open-mindedness, while ensuring genuine respect for their interests. We should listen to their complaints and their reasons and then seek a resolution of the conflict through discussion. Many problems can be minimised in this way and, in the long run, I believe this is the only way to deal effectively with the threat of terrorism.

QUESTION: How do you feel about returning to India with the threat of war hanging over that region?
THE DALAI LAMA: India is my second home, where I have spent 43 years of my life; so I have to return in spite of the looming threat of war. The relationship between Tibet and India goes back many centuries and is a unique and close one. I always describe it as a relationship between teacher and student; in this case, we Tibetans are the students and the Indians are our teachers.

When I first came to India, Pandit Jawaharlal Nehru

was Prime Minister. He personally took special care of us Tibetans, especially the education of the Tibetan refugee children. His basic policy on education for Tibetans has been adhered to by all successive prime ministers and governments of India, which has been extremely helpful for our community. So we really feel in our hearts that India is our home. In fact, right now, although physically I'm here and talking to you, my mind is already on the plane back to India. [Audience laughs.]

QUESTION: How can we help Tibet?

THE DALAI LAMA: One aspect of our problems has been due really to Chinese Government policy, which is based on a lack of awareness about Tibetan culture and history. A Chinese Government slogan states that one should 'seek truth from facts'. This is certainly a wise saying, but the facts have to be genuine facts, not falsehoods. Some of the local Chinese cadres in Tibet submit false reports out of a desire to please their superiors. Of course, any policy based on these false facts leads to disaster.

In 1973, as a result of discussions among a small group of Tibetans, I made up my mind that sooner or later we would need to find a solution to the Tibetan crisis through dialogue with the Chinese Government. I realised that the question of independence for Tibetans would not be realistic and accordingly formulated the idea of a 'middle way' approach. So in early 1979 my personal emissary had a meeting with Deng Xiaoping, the then Chairman of the Chinese Communist Party; at this meeting the Chinese leader stated that, apart from the question of Tibet's independence, anything could be discussed.

All our efforts since then have been within the framework laid down by Deng Xiaoping at that important meeting. Despite criticism from within the Tibetan community, criticism from some of our friends and supporters, public accusations against me by the Chinese Government, and the worsening situation in Tibet, I am still fully committed to the middle way approach. However, in spite of this, the Chinese Government repeatedly declares that the Dalai Lama is a 'splittist' and a 'separatist'. They make such accusations against me either out of fear or out of ignorance.

So whenever you have the opportunity to meet some of our Chinese brothers and sisters, tell them your feelings and try to discuss these issues with them, so that they can become better informed. More and more Chinese people are supporting Tibet these days and showing genuine sympathy and concern. Over the last few years I have received many communications from Chinese scholars, artists and writers. Such genuine concern and support is borne out of a better awareness of the situation.

Also, I want to tell you, as our supporters, that despite the lack of response from the Chinese Government side, we continue to persist in our struggle and campaign for the protection of the Tibetan environment, Tibetan culture, human rights and religious freedom. Looking from the wider perspective I'm optimistic about Tibet's future, because China is in a process of change. Sooner or later the People's Republic of China has to join the global trend of greater respect for human rights, respect for the right of self-determination and the rule of law, democracy, openness, freedom of speech, freedom of religious faith and freedom of the press.

But of course when we look locally at conditions inside Tibet, things are really terrible. Underneath the superficial progress that we see are so many problems and sad developments in terms of damage to Tibetan culture. When I am asked to comment on the situation in a few words I usually say that, whether intentionally or unintentionally, some kind of cultural genocide is taking place in Tibet.

Environmentally, the large-scale deforestation and indiscriminate mining in Tibet are seriously damaging Tibet's fragile ecology. And the transfer of ethnic Chinese people to Tibet is increasing by the month. Tibetans have already become a minority in our capital city of Lhasa and their lifestyle has changed radically, even their language: they are compelled to speak Chinese. When we look at Tibet locally like this the situation seems almost hopeless, but if we look at the situation from a wider global perspective it's more hopeful.

So please continue to support us, but not in an anti-Chinese way. In actual fact, support for the Tibetan cause is ultimately beneficial to the People's Republic of China itself. The present situation is bad for China's overall stability and unity, which I think are priorities for the Chinese Government. If China grants Tibet a meaningful autonomy, then genuine stability and unity will be the result.

So your support in finding a meaningful solution is of major benefit to China as well as Tibet, and you should not consider this an anti-Chinese struggle. Also, I don't think of your support for Tibet as pro-Tibetan; rather I see it as pro-justice, because the cause of Tibet is a just cause. Thank you.

Glossary

Abhidharma Literally meaning 'higher knowledge', Abhidharma refers to a collection of Buddhist scriptures that pertain to psychology, phenomenology and cosmology.

anatman Literally meaning 'no-self', anatman refers to an important Buddhist teaching according to which any notion of an eternal principle that is thought to constitute the real self of our existence is rejected.

arhat Literally 'foe destroyer', arhat refers to a person who has destroyed her or his delusions and is freed from cyclic existence.

arya A noble one who has attained high levels of spiritual realisation, especially direct insight into the ultimate nature of reality.

Atisha An eleventh century Indian Buddhist scholar, who was invited to Tibet by the king of Ngari. He is credited with reviving Buddhism in Tibet. A prolific writer and renowned teacher, he composed the *Lamp for the Path to Enlightenment*, the original prototype for the *lam rim* teachings.

bhumi (Skt) The ten stages that bodhisattvas progressively move through on the path to enlightenment. Also known as the ten grounds or paths.

bodhicitta Literally 'buddha mind'. The wish to practise compassion and altruism with the aim of relieving the sufferings of others.

bodhisattva Someone who possesses the compassionate motivation of bodhicitta, and devotes their life towards the achievement of enlightenment for the sake of all beings by practising the six perfections of giving, ethics, patience, enthusiastic effort, mental stabilisation and wisdom.

Buddha The first of the Three Jewels of refuge. A buddha is a fully enlightened being. The historical Buddha was Prince Siddhartha Gautama or Buddha Shakyamuni, who lived in India 600 BCE.

Buddhadharma The teachings (Dharma) of the Buddha.

buddhahood The state of perfect awakening, the attainment of which results in the individual becoming a buddha, an Awakened One. The perfection of wisdom and compassion.

buddha nature The seed of perfect enlightenment that is believed to naturally exist in all beings according to Mahayana Buddhism.

calm abiding meditation (See **shamatha**.)

Chenrezig (Tib.) Known as Avalokiteshvara in Sanskrit. A male aspect of a deity symbolising compassion and altruism, Chenrezig is depicted with four or 1000 arms. The Dalai Lama is considered to be a living embodiment of Chenrezig in our time.

compassion The altruistic wish to help free all beings from misery and suffering.

cyclic existence (See **samsara**.)

Dalai Lama The temporal and spiritual leader of the Tibetan people, in Tibet and in exile. The present Dalai Lama is the fourteenth. The title Dalai Lama means 'Ocean of Wisdom'.

deity A figure used in meditation, visualisation or tantra; a manifestation or representation of enlightened or buddha mind.

deity yoga The practice of visualising oneself as the deity, after receiving the initiation from a qualified teacher who holds the lineage.

Dharma The second of the Three Jewels of refuge. The spiritual teachings of the Buddha.

dharmakaya The 'truth body' or the 'Buddha body of reality'. This is the natural state of the Buddha's awakened mind, which is also its ultimate nature. (See **kaya**.)

eight mundane concerns The eight mundane concerns refer to a pair of four concerns that tend to dominate ordinary beings' normal state. They are 1) being delighted when praised and being dejected when belittled, 2) being delighted when one possesses something and being dejected when not possessing it, 3) being delighted when hearing pleasant words and being dejected when hearing unpleasant words, and 4) being delighted when prosperous and being dejected when suffering misfortune.

emptiness (See **shunyata**.)

enlightenment The fully awakened, realised and omniscient mind, pure and cleared of all obscurations. In Buddhism every being is capable of evolving to such an enlightened state by gradually transforming their mind.

Four Noble Truths The Buddha's first teaching in India was the Four Noble Truths, which is the foundation of Buddhist thought and practice. The Four Noble Truths are: the truth of suffering, the origin of suffering, the cessation of suffering and the path to the cessation of suffering.

Gelugpa The most recent of the four lineages of Tibetan Buddhism. Established by Lama Tsong Khapa in the fourteenth century.

geshe Meaning 'spiritual friend' in Tibetan, a geshe is a teacher in the Gelug tradition who has completed formal training and attained the geshe degree.

guru A spiritual teacher or mentor. (See **lama**.)

initiation (Tib. *wang*, Skt *abhisheka*) An empowerment bestowed by a qualified teacher giving permission to the student to join the family of practitioners and perform practices associated with a meditational deity.

Kagyu One of the four lineages of Tibetan Buddhism. His Holiness the seventeenth Karmapa, recently exiled in India after a childhood in Tibet, is head of this lineage.

Kalachakra The 'Wheel of Time' tantric system, which includes instructions on medicine, astronomy, time, yoga and physiology, encompassing the entire universe and the path to enlightenment. The Dalai Lama taught on the Kalachakra in Sydney in 1996. It is frequently connected with the promotion of world peace.

karma Literally meaning 'deed' in Sanskrit, karma refers to the law of cause and effect; of actions having consequences for oneself and others.

kaya Buddha's body or embodiment. (See **dharmakaya**.)

lama Literally meaning 'none higher', lama refers to someone who can be trusted as a teacher or spiritual friend and guide. One who is qualified to bestow empowerments and show by example the path to enlightenment. (See **guru**.)

Lama Tsong Khapa A fourteenth century teacher, writer and one of Tibet's great philosophers. He founded the Gelugpa (or Gelug) lineage of Tibetan Buddhism.

lojong Thought transformation, or training the mind. Comprises techniques for bringing the demands of the ego back into perspective and transforming thoughts or actions with altruistic intent, in order to reduce the self-cherishing mind and to be able to genuinely assist others.

lower realms Cyclic existence is divided into six realms: three of favourable birth and three of unfavourable birth. The three realms of unfavourable birth are referred to as the lower realms and these include the hell realms. Rebirth within cyclic existence is determined by one's accumulated karma.

Madhyamika The most influential of the four major philosophical schools of Indian Buddhism, based on the *Perfection of Wisdom Sutras* of Shakyamuni Buddha and founded by Nagarjuna. The term means 'Middle Way', taking the path between the extremes of nihilism and eternalism, using the wisdom or realisation of emptiness.

mahamudra Literally meaning 'great seal', mahamudra refers to a profound system of meditative practice where the primary focus is the nature of mind itself.

Mahayana Meaning the 'Great Vehicle', this system of Buddhism promotes reaching the goal of enlightenment not just to achieve nirvana for oneself, but in order to rescue all other beings from suffering. Mahayana offers a radical critique of everything we usually take seriously as existing independently, and a confidence that enlightenment is possible. Japan, China, Korea, Mongolia, Tibet, Bhutan and Vietnam follow Mahayana Buddhism. (See **Theravada**.)

mandala A circle or wheel representing the universe or the dwelling of a deity. When used symbolically they take the form of a two-dimensional image on cloth or an image made of coloured sand, or they may also be constructed as a three-dimensional image. The visualisation of a mandala plays a crucial role in tantric meditation.

Manjushri The Buddha of Wisdom.

mantra Literally 'that which protects the mind', a mantra is the recitation of primal syllables and is associated with a deity or practice.

meditation A disciplined mental process whereby one becomes familiar with different states of mind using various techniques such as breathing, visualisation and single-pointed concentration. A method to subdue, clear and train the mind.

Middle Way (See **Madhyamika**.)

moksha Literally meaning 'freedom', moksha refers to the attainment of liberation whereby the individual has achieved total freedom from suffering and its origins. In Buddhism moksha is equivalent to nirvana, which is the total cessation of suffering and its conditions.

mudra Hand gestures symbolising various activities; part of the Buddhist utilisation of body, speech and mind in harmony.

Nagarjuna A second-century AD Indian scholar and writer. One of his most famous works is the *Precious Garland*, a manual of advice for individuals as well as social and governmental policy. Nagarjuna propounded the Madhyamika or Middle Way school of emptiness.

nirmanakaya The Buddha's emanation body, which is the physical embodiment of the Buddha that is visible to the ordinary beings, such as human beings. The historical Buddha Shakyamuni is an example of such an emanation body Buddha.

nirvana The state of freedom from all suffering, delusions and karma, called the 'liberation from samsara' in the Tibetan tradition.

non-dual wisdom The wisdom directly realising emptiness, which is said to be non-dual in that it is free of all forms of duality like subject and object, identity and difference, and so on.

Nyingma The oldest of the four lineages of Tibetan Buddhism. Based on teachings introduced from India by Padmasambhava and others, as distinguished from the second spread of teachings in the eleventh century.

Padmasambhava Literally meaning 'born of a lotus', Padmasambhava is also known as Guru Rinpoche. He formally established Buddhism in Tibet in the eighth century.

penetrative insight meditation Penetrative insight meditation refers to a discipline of meditation where the primary emphasis is on deep analysis as opposed to single-pointed absorption on a chosen object. (See **vipassana**.)

pratyekabuddha Literally meaning 'solitary realisers', pratyekabuddhas are disciples of the Buddha who, through following the path of the 'lesser vehicle', chose to seek enlightenment primarily on the basis of self-reliance.

rebirth The continuum of aspects of the mind after death, which seek embodiment again according to the karma accumulated in past lives.

refuge There are three objects of refuge in Buddhism — the Buddha, the Dharma, and Sangha, which is the spiritual community. Going for refuge in these three implies entrusting one's spiritual well-being to the Buddha as the teacher, the Dharma as the true source of refuge, and the community as the support while one is on the path.

Rinpoche Literally meaning 'precious one', this is the title given to someone formally recognised as the reincarnation of a past lama or teacher.

rupakaya The Buddha's form body, namely the embodied form of a fully awakened one that is visible to other beings.

sadhana The practice and instructions given when taking on a commitment associated with a meditational deity. A liturgy used in daily devotions.

Sakya One of the four lineages of Tibetan Buddhism.

sambhogakaya The 'enjoyment body' or the 'Buddha body of perfect resource'. Sambhogakaya is the extremely subtle state of the Buddha's physical embodiment, which, according to the texts, is perceptible only to bodhisattvas on high levels of spiritual realisation.

Samkhya school An ancient Indian philosophical school of thought.

samsara Cyclic existence, the wheel of continuous death and rebirth.

Sangha The Buddhist community, or ordained monks and nuns. The third of the Three Jewels of refuge.

Sanskrit The most important language of classical India; it is the language in which many of the Buddhist texts were originally written.

sentient being Any living being with consciousness that is not free from gross and subtle ignorance.

Seven Limb Practice A popular ritual in Mahayana Buddhism. The seven limbs are making prostrations, offering, purifying negativity, rejoicing, requesting the Buddhas to turn the Wheel of Dharma, appealing to the Buddhas not to enter into final nirvana, and, finally, dedication.

shamatha Calm abiding meditation. A state of mind which is characterised by the stabilisation of attention on an internal object of observation, combined with the calming of external distractions to the mind.

Shantideva A well-known seventh century Buddhist teacher who wrote the great Mahayana classic *Guide to the Bodhisattva's Way of Life.*

shravaka Literally meaning 'listener', shravaka refers to the disciples of the Buddha whose primary concern in their spiritual path is to gain freedom from suffering for themselves and to follow the path of the 'lesser vehicle'.

shunyata Translated as 'emptiness', meaning the absence of any abiding essence in things or in the contents of the mind, the insubstantiality of whatever seems solid and enduring. To realise shunyata as the condition of all human existence is to become free, by cutting the source of suffering at its root. (See **ultimate truth** and **wisdom**.)

skilful means This refers to such altruistic practices as cultivation of compassion and loving kindness, complemented with the wisdom of emptiness in Mahayana Buddhism.

suchness An epithet for emptiness, which refers to the way things really are.

Sutras The teachings or scriptures of Buddha Shakyamuni.

svabhavakaya One of the two aspects of dharmakaya that pertain to the natural state of the Buddha's enlightened mind.

tantra Refers to the Vajrayana or 'Diamond Vehicle'. The inner teachings of Mahayana Buddhism, used to progress rapidly on the path to enlightenment. Tantric practice succeeds if the practitioner has first developed considerable concentration, steadiness, equanimity and insight. Requires confidence and dedication.

Tara A female meditational deity who is regarded as the embodiment of all the buddha's enlightened activity. There are many different aspects of Tara, the most popular of these are Green Tara (mainly associated with protection) and White Tara (often associated with healing and longevity practices).

Tathagata An epithet of the Buddha, which literally means 'He who has gone thus.'

thangka A scroll painting which depicts deities or illustrations, such as the Wheel of Life, and is used for visualisation and meditational purposes. An external representation of what the meditator internalises and imaginatively interacts with.

Theravada The Buddhism of India, Sri Lanka, Burma, Laos, Thailand and Cambodia.

Three Higher Trainings Higher training in morality, higher training in concentration and higher training in wisdom, which together constitute the heart of the Buddhist path to enlightenment.

Three Jewels The Buddha, Dharma and Sangha as the teacher, the teachings and the community of practitioners respectively.

tonglen An important Buddhist practice of training one's mind towards great compassion and altruism. Tonglen, which literally means 'giving and taking', refers to a specific visualisation practice wherein practitioners mentally give away all their positive factors to other beings, while taking upon themselves all the sufferings of others and the conditions that lead them to suffer.

Tripitaka Literally meaning 'the three baskets', the *Tripitaka* refers to the three main scriptural collections attributed to the Buddha, these being the collections on morality, concentration and wisdom.

Twelve Links of Dependent Origination Ignorance, volition, consciousness, name and form, sources, contact, feeling, craving, grasping, becoming, birth, and ageing and death. According to Buddhism, it is through an interlocking chain of these twelve factors that an individual wanders within the cycle of unenlightened existence.

two accumulations Accumulation of merit and accumulation of wisdom; the perfection of which culminates in the attainment of perfect buddhahood in Mahayana Buddhism.

ultimate truth The ultimate truth refers to the ultimate nature of reality, which according to Mahayana Buddhism is understood in terms of the doctrine of emptiness, namely the absence of intrinsic existence of all things. It is one of the Two Truths, the other being the conventional truth.

Vajrayana The 'Diamond Vehicle'. The most intensive path to enlightenment, requiring a grounding in meditative concentration and insight. (See **tantra**.)

view A conscious knowledge of Buddhism as a path. A perspective which penetrates to the heart of reality. Study of the teachings as a coherent system for attaining happiness. Along with meditation and action, they comprise the three foundations of Buddhism.

Vinaya (Skt) Literally meaning 'discipline', the Vinaya is the code of monastic discipline and ethics for ordained Sangha (monks and nuns).

vipassana Otherwise called 'penetrative insight meditation', vipassana refers to an analytical meditative state penetrating the nature, characteristics and function of the object of the meditation, accompanied by physical and mental suppleness of the body and mind and generated on the basis of calm abiding. Also spelled 'vipasyana'.

wisdom Realisation of the insubstantiality or emptiness of everything that appears to us, internal or external. (See also **shunyata** and **vipassana**.)

Yogacara An alternative Sanskrit name for the Mind Only school of Mahayana Buddhism. Two key founders of this school are the two brothers, Asanga and Vasubandhu.

yogi Solitary practitioner: often meditating in retreat, in forests or caves, unconstrained by convention; or wandering in society speaking truths, singing spontaneous songs of realisation and fulfilling the wishes of others.

Endnotes

1 The understanding or realisation of emptiness is discussed in chapters three and four.

2 For a brief explanation of the thirty-seven aspects of the path to enlightenment, see H.H. the Dalai Lama, *The World of Tibetan Buddhism*, Wisdom Publications, Boston, 1995, pp. 20–2.

3 These are the perfections of generosity, ethical discipline, forbearance, joyous effort, concentration and wisdom.

4 *Fundamentals of the Middle Way*, chapter 24, verse 18. All translations from the Tibetan sources are Geshe Thupten Jinpa's unless otherwise stated. For an alternative translation of this verse, see Jay L. Garfield, *The Fundamental Wisdom of the Middle Way*, Oxford University Press, New York, 1995, p. 69.

5 *Guide to the Bodhisattva's Way of Life*, chapter 8, verse 130. For an alternative translation, see *The Bodhicaryavatara*, The World's Classics, Oxford University Press, New York, 1996, p. 99.

6 Verses copyright © 2000 His Holiness the Dalai Lama, *Transforming the Mind: Teachings on Generating Compassion* (edited and translated by Geshe Thupten Jinpa), Thorsons, HarperCollins Publishers, London, 2000. Copyright in the customised version vests in Lothian Books.

7 The ten negative actions are: (of the body) killing, stealing and sexual misconduct; (of speech) lying, idle chatter, slander and harsh speech; (of the mind) covetousness, ill will and wrong views. The ten positive actions are the opposite of these.

8 This is a passage from a scripture quoted by Chandrakirti in his auto-commentary to *Entering the Middle Way*.

9 *Entering the Middle Way*, chapter 6, verse 120.

10 For a detailed description and explanation of the Buddhist teaching on the Twelve Links of Dependent Origination, see H.H. the Dalai Lama, *Meaning of Life: Buddhist Perspectives on Cause and Effect*, Wisdom Publications, Boston, 1992.

11 *Guide to the Bodhisattva's Way of Life*, chapter 8, verse 131. For an alternative translation of the verse, see *The Bodhicaryavatara*, The World's Classics, Oxford University Press, New York, 1996, p. 100.

12 For a detailed and accessible exposition by the Dalai Lama on this twelfth-century Tibetan spiritual classic, see *Awakening the Mind, Lightening the Heart*, HarperCollins, San Francisco, 1995.

13 The eight mundane concerns refer to a set of four opposite emotions in response to events: elated when praised and dejected when criticised; elated when hearing pleasant

words and dejected when hearing unpleasant words; elated when obtaining material gifts and dejected when denied material gifts; and, finally, elated when enjoying prosperity and dejected when experiencing misfortune.

14 The translation of Atisha's verses used in this chapter are reproduced with permission from *Atisha's Lamp for the Path to Enlightenment*, copyright © Geshe Sonam Rinchen (translated and edited by Ruth Sonam), Snow Lion Publications, New York, 1997. www.snowlionpub.com

15 *Four Hundred Verses on the Middle Way*, chapter 8, verse 15.

16 These are the animal realm, the realm of the *pretas* (hungry ghosts) and the hell realms.

17 Form and formless realms refer to higher levels of existence in the celestial realm, birth in which is described as the fruits of deep meditative absorptions that one has engaged in during one's life.

18 Cyclic existence refers to the perpetual cycle of birth and death known as samsara in Sanskrit.

19 The higher realms are those of humans, demi-gods and gods.

20 The remaining three characteristics are suffering, emptiness, and the absence of selfhood.

21 For a full description of this ceremony, see chapter three.

22 *Fundamentals of the Middle Way*, chapter 24, verse 10a. For an alternative translation of these two lines, see Jay L. Garfield, *The Fundamental Wisdom of the Middle Way*, Oxford University Press, New York, 1995, p. 68.

Recommended reading

WORKS BY HIS HOLINESS THE DALAI LAMA

Kindness, Clarity and Insight (translated and edited by Jeffrey Hopkins), Snow Lion Publications, New York, 1984.

The Meaning of Life: Buddhist Perspectives on Cause and Effect (translated by Jeffrey Hopkins), Wisdom Publications, Boston, 1992.

A Flash of Lightning in the Dark of Night: a Guide to the Bodhisattva's Way of Life (translated by the Padmakara Translation Group), Shambala, USA, 1994.

The Way to Freedom, The Library of Tibet (edited by Donald S. Lopez Jr), HarperCollins, San Francisco, 1994.

Awakening the Mind, Lightening the Heart, The Library of Tibet (edited by Donald S. Lopez Jr), HarperCollins, San Francisco, 1995.

The World of Tibetan Buddhism (translated by Geshe Thupten Jinpa), Wisdom Publications, Boston, 1995.

The Heart of the Buddha's Path (translated by Geshe Thupten Jinpa), Thorsons, London, 1999.

Ancient Wisdom, Modern World — Ethics for the New Millennium, Little, Brown & Co., London, 1999.

Transforming the Mind: Teachings on Generating Compassion (translated by Geshe Thupten Jinpa), Thorsons, HarperCollins Publishers, London, 2000.

OTHER WORKS

Acarya Nagarjuna, *The Precious Garland: An Epistle to a King* (translated by John Dunne and Sara McClintock), Wisdom Publications, Boston, 1997.

Geshe Sonam Rinchen, *Atisha's Lamp for the Path to Enlightenment* (translated and edited by Ruth Sonam), Snow Lion Publications, New York, 1997.

Geshe Sonam Rinchen, *Eight Verses on Training the Mind* (translated and edited by Ruth Sonam), Snow Lion Publications, New York, 2001.

Jay L. Garfield, *The Fundamental Wisdom of the Middle Way: Nagarjuna's Mulamadhyamakakarika*, Oxford University Press, New York, 1995.

Shantideva, *The Bodhicaryavatara*, The World's Classics (translated by Kate Crosby and Andrew Skilton), Oxford University Press, Oxford, 1996.

Acknowledgements

The Publisher would like to thank the following people and organisations who assisted with this book: His Holiness the Dalai Lama; Geshe Thupten Jinpa for his brilliant work translating and editing these teachings; the Tibet Information Office, Canberra; Chope Paljor Tsering; Ven. Lakdhor at the Office of His Holiness the Dalai Lama, Dharamsala; members of Dalai Lama in Australia Limited, especially Wendy White and Dr Alan Molloy; Vyvyan Cayley for editing and assisting Geshe Thupten Jinpa; HarperCollins Publishers for permission to reproduce Geshe Thupten Jinpa's translation of the *Eight Verses of Mind Training* from *Transforming the Mind: Teachings on Generating Compassion* © His Holiness the Dalai Lama; Snow Lion

Publications for permission to reproduce the verses from *Atisha's Lamp for the Path to Enlightenment* © Geshe Sonam Rinchen; Anna Carlile for the jacket design; Caz Brown for the internal design and typesetting; Steve Grimwade for editorial assistance; Alison Ribush and Mandala Books; photographers Greg Bartley, Sonja De Sterke, Deyan, Shane Rozario, Ross Schultz, Michael Silver and Jenny Templin.

Index

hachette
AUSTRALIA

If you would like to find out more about Hachette Australia, our authors, upcoming events and new releases you can visit our website or our social media channels:

hachette.com.au

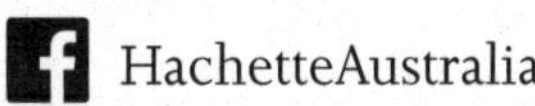

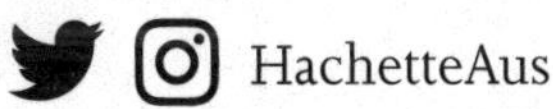